MADRIGALS,

SONGS AND SONNETS.

BY

JOHN ARTHUR BLAIKIE

AND

EDMUND WILLIAM GOSSE.

LONDON :

LONGMANS, GREEN, AND CO.

1870.

TO

MRS. HENRY CURTIS,

𝕿𝖍𝖎𝖘 𝕭𝖔𝖔𝖐

IS AFFECTIONATELY INSCRIBED.

CONTENTS.

SONNETS.

MADRIGALS.

MADRIGALS.

ST. CECILIA.

FORTH from the cloud-fring'd east,
Inwoven fair with cloudlets golden,
Like those Hesperian apples olden,
With sudden fire inflaming all the skies,
The sun uprose !—a luscious feast
To all who frighted Night with heavy cries
Of minds perplexed
By troubles vexed
Of Love, that echoed far a wild despair !

Now over dewy hill and dusky dale
His level beams do course,
With unresisted force,
Till, lo ! before a minster rare,

They fling on high a pale and mystic light,
From spire to spire, and on from height to
    height ;
And through the stainèd glass,
Flushing the massive organ as they pass,
They fall on one, who, fair and pale,
Before the chancel-rail
In adoration kneels.

A drowsy stillness held that minster old,
Until Cecilia, from her matins risen,
Beheld the sun, escapèd from his prison,
His streaming glories o'er the heavens unfold.
Then o'er the organ-keys she bends,
And forth there peals,
Waking on high the echoes loud and long,
The beauteous music of the Latin song ;
To which she lends,
With vigour fine,
The full-strain'd powers of a voice divine !

While yet the air is tremulous around,
With dying tones of slowly-ebbing sound,

Far from on high an angel flits,
With more than morning-light and freshness
    crown'd,
And mutely hovers where she silent sits,
Her gold hair flowing in the golden light,
Her rapt eyes lifted to the glow above,
Her whole soul gifted by supremest Love
To charm the night
To sudden flight
Through Music's all-eternal might.

THE POET TO NATURE.

FAR in the silence of the flowery west,
Mother, there lies a valley, only known
To me, thy child and worshipper, thine own !
Thither I wander'd in the idle quest
Of the shy ouzel's nest ;
And there I found
Thee, queen and goddess, most supremely
    crown'd
With leafy loveliness.
The calmness of a silver sunset fell
Upon thine eyes, so turn'd to amethyst,
Smiling on me ; and, first in that green dell,
I felt thy fingers press
My brows with ivy bound.

MUSIC.

BEFORE the clavichord
Stately she sat, and from her fine lips pour'd
The song I love so well :
Fair is she, yet I could afford
To lose those deep eyes where clear violets dwell,
And, in a whirl of sound,
To gain the heaven where her young spirit soar'd,
Forgetful of the ground.
Music, thy noblest servant, Israfel,
Feels not his lyre-heart more divinely bound
At seraph-chaunts, than I to hear
That passionate rondel throb with hope and fear !

THE LIGHT OF DEATH

Life lay long lingering in her heaven-lit eyes ;
Her breast heav'd not
Responding to our sighs,
Nor did her lips speak aught ;
Yet we, with glad surprise,
In soft faint whispers thus our fears allay'd :—
"Our love she knoweth, and therein she liveth ;
The Power that lent her life now giveth
A light unto her eyes that ne'er shall fade ! "

And when it failed from me,
Leaving its semblance in my mind for ever,
How fled ye then, ye chilly fears !
How thou returnedst, Hope, to cease, oh ! never
Thy lovely tale of hearts that cannot sever,
In realms serene high-lifted o'er the tears
That feed Time's sullen sea !

THE ANGEL OF THE ANNUNCIATION.

STILL, with the lightning speed of his swift flight,
The rainbows of his wings
Vibrated, and his hair bore still the light
That shone around it in those mansions bright,
Whence the sun's glory springs;
On one knee to the Virgin fair he bent,
And, in a low clear voice of silver chord,
Gave forth the mystic word
Wherewith he had been sent;
A choral murmur of rich music blent
With the faint echo; then from her rapt sight
He faded, unador'd.

SUNSET AND DAWN.

I. THE SUNSET.

"Give us thy peace, O Lord!"
So rang their solemn prayer,
Beneath the quaint carv'd roof;
For they had heard
Lov'd lips deal mild reproof
Unto their worldly care,
Their flitting faith, unfix'd,
Their trust with doubting mix'd;
Then, weary and convicted, they
Their burdens at His feet did lay,
Whom they in earnest, tearful tones implor'd :-
"Give us thy peace, O Lord!"
Ah, ne'er canst thou, nor I, dear love,

Forget that summer eve,
When we, our hearts borne far above
By Truth so dear and Love so great,
That village church did leave,
With all the first-dawn of the peace
Causing within our hearts to cease
The reign of Hate ;
When life's grim torturers, dread and drear,
False Doubt and Pride and coward Fear,
Fast fled away.

O blissful Day !
Thy setting sun with all its clouds did wear
A beauty all-transforming, soft and rare,
Whose rosy light across the western sea
Flew up the wooded hill from tree to tree,
And then up each green alley sent
A diadem all bright
Unto the hawthorns white,
Which beneath the sombre hue
Of that forest, upward grew,
Like saints in darkness seeking for the light ;
And there was lent

Unto the grass thy radiance and life,
And all the sward and sweet wild flowers,—
The lights of spring's fresh younger hours,—
Beneath the evening wind were rife
With tremulous waves of ever-mingling strife;
And to the zenith's blue
Thy flush upflew,
More broadly spreading as its flight rose higher;
And, 'twixt the dark old pines,
In trembling lines,
Went streaming swift in quivering rays of fire.

II. THE DAWN.

FAIR is God's earth, for ever fair
To all who Nature's reign do own,
And with pure hearts do oft repair
To bow before her mystic throne
With unaccusing thought and free:
But that sweet eve did we,
Our burden gone,
Our peace arising and our terrors flown,

Feel Nature's presence nigher
For One we knew diviner far and higher;
And our great joy did overflow,
And mingle in the sunset's glow,
And to the ocean-light give light,
And peace to stillness, strength to might,
In all the glory that the earth then wore,
The roseate sea and sky, the peaceful, silent
    shore.

In quiet once again,
But not in pain,—
While neither grief nor thought oppress'd
The sweet on-coming of the promis'd rest,—
Arose our solemn prayer,
" Give us, O Lord, Thy peace,
Take Thou, O Lord, our care !

" And when Death's dear release
On welcome wings shall come,
To bear us unto Thee who art our home,
May'st Thou who mak'st our present pain to
    cease,

Grant us in full to know
What now in part doth flow
To hearts outpour'd,—
Thy peace made perfect, Lord,
Thy perfect peace ! "

OPHELIA.

" She was as white as the lily flower."
Knight of the Burning Pestle

WHERE didst thou find thy love?

Among the lilies, that, golden-spik'd and white,
Bend over the still lake, and catch the light
On ivory petals as they move.—
Among the lilies; and her hair was bright
With the dull sheeny splendour of wet gold,
And all her flesh was cold.
Then from the calm grey heavens above
A summer-evening light shone down, and night
Came ere I was aware.—
White and gold, like the lilies, calm and fair,
And moving like the lilies, waved or roll'd
By the capricious air.

SYLVIA.

(In the early manner.)

Down beside a hillock green,
In sunlit rushes' silvery sheen,
Sylvia fair did sit,
Sylvia the fair !
And whispering zephyrs past her flit,
The while she combs her glistening hair,
And whisper amorous tales
Of life within the dales.
But Coridon did sport with love,
And in the scented brake
The leaves with sighs did shake ;
But she he loved with all above,
Viewing in fright the coming night,
With feet now dry took sudden flight,

And by that hillock green,
And in that silvery sheen,
By Coridon (the simple shepherd swain !)
Was never seen again.

"Ay me ! my love, though pure as light
Sleeping on beds of snow,
With blushing all a-glow,
Has frighted into seemly shame
Her (alas !) whose very name
To brightness chang'd the night,
And eased my troubled sprite."
Ah ! fond and fool, (quoth Love,) nor hot
    nor cold,
None ever yet lost love though overbold.

AN INVITATION.

COME to the river-bank with me ;
For there are plumèd ferns of crescent green,
And in the wine-dark pools are seen
The crimson-spotted trout.
Hush ! hush ! move through the brake most
    silently,
Vex with no loud unhallow'd shout
The holy secrecy of this sweet glade,
And you shall see
The dipper rush with sudden flash, and fade
Into the woodland screen ;
Nor shall you by your presence make afraid
The kingfisher, who looks down dreamily
At his own shadow gorgeously array'd.

HAMPSTEAD, 1869.

AGAINST the purple evening-light most dark
The old church tower stood,
Steep'd in a silence that was eloquent,
Within a gold irradiated flood,—
The sun's o'erflowing glory !
Nor could I mark
Or life or moving breath
As Night with owl-like rush, embracing, bent
Across the sullen heath,·
Save when the leaves, dying and pale and hoary,
Stirr'd 'twixt each quiet mound
With rustling sound.
But with the night there came
One who did break my numbèd heart to tears,
Raising my hopes, dispelling all my fears,

c 2

Who told, beneath the stars, the thrilling story
Of him whose name unites in Love's strong bands
The loveliest of all poetic lands,
Green-wreathèd England, sunny Italy !
Whose memory, like the Delphic flame,
'Twixt all blue skies and fair ethereal seas,
But more upon this heath and mid these trees,
Burneth eternally.

THE CRY OF THE UNSATISFIED.

O sing, sweet lark, some calmer, sadder song!
Thy melody awakes
A grief unsuited to the dawn and thee ;
My heart, my poor heart breaks !
Its pain doth foully wrong
The golden glory of the sun-lit sea ;
The long fields sloping to the ridg'd sea-sand
Take up the light, and send it through the land.
Above their waving grain I hear and see,
Climbing the air with ardent wings,
Thy spirit-form that shouts and sings,
Enraptur'd with the joy the scarlet sunrise brings.
But I,
Forgetting all the morning-grace,
And hiding in the chill sand-drift my face,

MADRIGALS.

Moan out, " O night, too, too soon dead,
Oh! whither art thou fled?
Be silent, lark, or soar so high
Thy notes may fade away and die ;
Let, rather, from yon tamarisk-grove,
The nightingale, that lover-bird,
Sing low of unrequited love
In strains more sweet and sad than cold Earth
    ever heard ! "

A SPRING SORROW.

THIS morn I linger'd long
Beside the alders tall that gleam
Across the stream ;
And grief did make the warbler's song
And all the sunny life of early May,
So blithe and gay,
A heavy dream ;
Whilst Faith aye strove
In vain, alas ! to reach the Love
That ruleth in eternal fulness strong.

For one, my Heart of hearts, whose life,
With all its hope and innocence,
Is as a spring in everlasting strife
With this cold world,

Lay low in pain, indued with little sense
Of all the bliss and glow,
The blue above, the radiant green below,
By Spring unfurl'd.

May He, who trod the furnace fierce
With three who dared the Babylonish death,
Enable her to pierce
The heavy clouds by mortal anguish rais'd,
That in this fiery trial of her faith
She may find Him with low and gentle voice
With her sad spirit walking ever nigh,
And with His comfort bidding her rejoice ;
That she, renewèd from on high,
As if on Him, her Saviour, she had gaz'd,
To me may come,
A calm and happy soul unapt to rove ;
Completing all our joy in this sweet home,
Amid these wooded glades,
With tearful memories of the care and love
Of Him who rears for us a home above,
That never fades !

TINTAGEL

On the dark ridges of the granite steep
I stood in thought, above the moaning sea,
While spirits of the unweary deep
In sun and wind were swathing me ·
Round me no mirth nor human jollity
Broke the great solemn silence; yet I knew
An awful joy went throbbing through
Each ledge of rock, each curl of rippling foam .
Then to *my* soul the thrilling gladness flew,
And I shall bear through years to come,
Hid in dim avenues of memory,
The splendour of that visionary sleep

SALMACIS.

By the cruel art of Love dismay'd,
In pain, I lay within a covert wild,
Under the green-spread shade ;
Beside a lovely fount that play'd,
Its waters gushing with a bubbling sound,
Adown a gentle dell with lilies bound ;
And in my sleep a veiling mild
Across my eyelids tremblingly was thrown ;
And lo ! athwart that fountain's brim there shone
The light from two bright eyes of blue
Gleaming in love most true ;—
Sweet Salmacis it was in piteous tears !
As she upon the chilly waters gaz'd,
Oh ! how I wept and joinèd in her fears,
Feeling with her amaz'd
To be unsatisfied ;
" Ah me, O happy nymph !" I cried anon,
" Thy Love and thou are by the gods made one ;
But she I love is made by them a stone,
A statue proud, and cold and deified !"

EROS TO PSYCHE.

REMEMBER not, O Love! the days gone by,
Nor, blushing, stand and sigh!
Hold up once more the clear memorial flame
Within the purple hollow of the night;
And let the glow flush all thy rosy limbs,
As once most mournfully!
Ah! chase the dew that dims
Thine eyes made heavy-lidded with old shame;
We will forget the pale twilight
Of the old love that died so wretchedly :
And this shall be the golden splendid dawn
Of deeper ecstasy than ever came
Round my dread mother's path through Paphos'
    lawn.

SANTA LUCIA.

O LORD, my lovers gaze into my eyes,
But I am blind to any love but thine ;
I will not cramp my soul with carnal ties,
Nor soil that passion, saintly and divine.
Another path is mine :—
Austere and chaste to thee I would arise ;
And now, within this chapel on the hill,
Girdled with pine-woods, sung to by all winds,
My throbbing heart is still,
Calm'd with the rest it finds ;
Around me, when I wake, the dawning sings ,
I join all nature in the choral hymn ;
And, sitting here alone,
All heaven grows scarlet with the seraph's wings ,
And, past the choirs of blue-eyed cherubim,
I gaze far up to Thy immortal throne !

LYRICS.

STANZAS.

Ah! well 'tis the semblance
  Of Love comes to thee,
Destroying remembrance
  Of falsehood to me :
He'll spread out the lightness
  Of Lethean wings ;
Thou'lt live in the brightness,
  Unheeding the stings.

Yet there they lie hidden,
  Soon, too soon, to rise,
Unsought and unbidden,
  To dim thy fair eyes ;

To make each To-morrow
  Repeat a To-day
Of unresting sorrow
  And cruel dismay.

Did I, when Love left me,
  With thee taking flight,
Feel he had bereft me
  Of all of his light,
Well might I my measure
  Of ill wishes add
To the evil-fraught treasure
  In which thou art glad.

I call not the angels,
  With mystical lays
And glowing evangels
  Of halcyon days,
To bring to thy spirit
  The life of the past,
That thou should'st inherit
  With me the fierce blast.

For Love once embower'd
   Within my lone heart,—
Though the cloud now hath lower'd,
   And he doth depart,—
Leaves a sensible presence,
   I own and I feel,—
A spiritual essence
   To strengthen and heal.

And all of thee faithless,
   And all of thee weak,
Though remembrance is deathless,
   And passion not meek,—
Are lost in the glory
   Of Beauty far-seen.
I live in the story
   Of love that hath been.

D

IANTHE

" I ENTER thy garden, my lover, my spouse,
   I breathe the faint odour of pale daffodils,
     I have gathered a leaf from the heart of the rose
Art thou there, O my darling, my light of the house,
   The house that is dark in the cup of the hills?
     Look out to me now ere the river-breeze blows '"

Her window is open to let the cool air
   Fan refreshingly brows that the noon-day made tir'd,
     She sleeps! in the silence I fancy I hear
Her low-breathed whispers the calm night-winds bear;
   And I see o'er the lintel her white arm attir'd
     In the withering curl'd tendrils of vine-leaves
       grown sere

Still she sleeps!   "O beloved, I knock at the door
    Of thy heart with emotion : O rise, let me in !
        Let the dreams with swift wings from thy slumber
            fly far !"
And I trill a low harmony never before
    Sung by aught but one bird in this desert of sin,—
        By the nightingale taught by the soul of a star.

As I cease she awakens ; I hear in the calm
    That small golden head on the white pillow turn ;
        A short sigh—and a pause, while her heart made
            aware
Of my presence throbs silently ;—then in the balm
    Of her chamber full motion, and while my eyes burn
        To receive such a glory, she smiles on me there.

But I stay in the dusk of the cedar awhile,
    Till she leans out inquiringly into the night ;
        I linger to drink the full beauty of her,
Who, as now she looks lovingly down with a smile,
    Is more fair than the dawn, and more dear than the
           light,
        Whose hair drops with spikenard, her fingers with
           myrrh.

Then I pass from the shadow, made bold by my love,
   And hold her sweet lips to my mouth in a kiss ,
     And there in the garden, in silent delight,
Breast to breast we hang speechless ; nor mark where
      above
   The vigilant stars are aware of all this,
     Yet are gracious, and mar not the bliss of that
     night.

AN ELEGY OF THE SUMMER TIME.

ALAS, alas ! that thou shouldst fade !
   That all thy happy beauty lies,
(Now Death's swift call hath been obey'd)
    'Neath summer skies !

That 'tis in vain one lovely glade
   In summer's deepest leafage lies,
Where thou, so oft, hast happy play'd,
    With laughing eyes !

For nevermore shall come to me
   Thy laugh, dear child, upon the wind :
Thy hope and fear alike to me
    Are left behind :

No more thou'lt greet, and rear, and tend,
   The dumb companions of thy mirth ,
Oh ! would that thou couldst to them lend
    Quick flight from earth !

They do but tell me of my loss,
   As if they added new to new,
Fresh pangs to anguish, cross to cross,
    With aim too true !

In vain for thee the noonday sun
   Makes cool and fresh thy arbour rare :
No more in glee thou'lt leap and run,
    A child of air !

Bare Winter never found thee here ,
   And where thou wast, ah ! who can tell ?
Silent and sad, as leaf all sere,
    Within thy cell.

But when the swallows came, outflew
   A summer child, a lightsome form,
What time late April odours blew,
    And past the storm.

This eve is thine, and for thee made!
  O what spring-swallow, swift and gay,
Will bring thee to me, ne'er to fade,
    Thou sunny fay?

Thou'lt ne'er return!—and my great loss
  Must aye be borne in thought of thee,
Until I come myself to cross
    Death's dreary sea.

DROWNED IN DART.

REQUIESCAT ! let her lie
　Where the river bubbles by ;
Where, in endless prophesying
　Of the bliss she shall inherit,
Never thought of death or dying
　Can disturb her sleeping spirit.
　　Requiescat ! Let her lie,
　　In embalming sanctity,
　　Where the bubbles tremble by.

　Resurgetque ! she shall rise,
　Light revisit those cold eyes ;
Waves dissever, not for ever,
　Her sweet spirit and our love ;
We shall meet, to part, ah ! never,
　In the paradise above.
　　Resurgemus ! we shall rise !
　　Though now ashy-pale she lies,
　　Life shall visit those cold eyes !

A LIFE'S LYRIC.

I.

With hearts of youth in the well of truth
  My Love and I went diving,
Like the banded bees, 'gainst the winds that freeze
  Sweet thoughts and joys a hiving.

Naught cared we then for the world of men,
  Knowing nor good nor evil,
As glowing we lay, 'neath the blushing May,
  A watching the ocean-level.

And she so light took my heart and sight
  With love-tones and faery-wiles,
While the wing'd days flew o'er the waters blue,
  Each radiant alike with smiles.

II.

But the doubt came in ; and then the sin
    Of Pride came on apace,
Making scenes so cheery a wilderness dreary,
    Blasted by passions base.

I knew that her pride was sorely tried
    By the love of one like me :—
But oh ! that such leaven should mar such a heaven,
    That summer alone by the sea !

And now it is flown ; nor sigh, nor groan,
    E'er brings to my spirit relief :
Though my anger is past, her scorn doth last
    As lasting (ah me !) as my grief.

III.

" O let not my cry, O Love most high,
    Add to thy scorn thy hate ! "
So runs my bewailing, like an empty wailing
    Whose burden is " late—too late ! "

" No more can I view the ocean blue,
　　Nor the blossom of hawthorn bright,
Nor sail in the skiff, nor mount the green cliff,
　　Without thought of the lonely night,

" When I left thee for aye, and thou wert gay,
　　And lightsome with jest and laughing,—
As before the death-shock a man may mock
　　The wailing of Grief with scoffing !"

IV.

Near the sandy rim of ocean dim,—
　　A hot and forsaken shore,—
Where on still spring-nights mid the wooded heights
　　Is heard the nightingale's lore ;

Near a dingle sweet where trees do meet
　　The zephyrs in wavy commotion,
Is a marble shrine oft kiss'd by the brine
　　Of an Elysian and eastern ocean ;

And over this tomb grows the red may-bloom,
   As Love in the end may cover
By a late relenting, the humble repenting
   And death and despair of a lover!

A MADONNA OF 1310.

SHE is stiff and thin, but the eyes at least
   Shine with an earnest love and true ;
Though the brows and nose, it must be confess'd,
   Are formal and hard ; while the sweet mouth too
Stiffens with gravity, where should float
   A smile to take hearts unaware ;
Yet I can fancy a carolling note
   Making those white lips rosy and fair !

Was not this lady, with great gold crown,
   And drapery heavy with gems, and straight,
Whose massive aureole presses down
   Her lank hair like a metal plate,—
Some sweet Italian girl, whose eye,
   While she sang right blithely down the street,
Flash'd up at Giotto suddenly,
   As she tripp'd away on her light hind's feet ?

May we not think, as I love to dream,
   That the painter,—tir'd with the weary work
Of making the saints and angels seem
   (Though a dim despair in his heart would lurk)
At least a little like flesh and blood,—
   Looking away in vague desire,
Suddenly caught, from where he stood,
   That face, and his artist soul flash'd fire,

And yearn'd, with love unsatisfied,
   To frame in colour that lovely face,
And its phantom, ever by his side,
   Look'd up to him with an aery grace ,
Though, for one moment, and never again,
   Her soul had pierc'd his through and through,
Those eyes return'd with a weary pain,
   There was flame to scorch in their pure bright blue

Till at last in anger he seiz'd the brush,
   And work'd away with his own firm hand,
While this passion made the life-blood rush
   Back to his heart, and half-unmann'd

His stalwart arm ;—but the phantom-eyes
   Kept him alert, and the picture grew
Under his hand, till with sad surprise
   He paus'd, and nothing was left to do.

Then, as he laid the colours by,
   In came a scholar-friend, no doubt,
And started and flush'd delightedly,
   And hail'd this triumph of Art with a shout.
Florence and all her great and wise
   Buzz'd and flutter'd around and prais'd
Giotto the while with troubled eyes
   Ruefully over his picture gaz'd ;

Nothing replied, and let them admire .—
   " The finest painting the world has seen !
Our Cimabue could never aspire
   To this our Giotto's golden mean,
So he died, as was best ! "   But he silently sigh'd,
   And thought of the sun-bright face, and knew,
When Man his loftiest art has tried,
   He but learns how much there is left to do !

COWPER AT MUNDSLEY.

During the winter of 1795, which Cowper spent at Mundsley, he walked much by the sea, endeavouring vainly to throw off the dejection which now more than ever oppressed him

WHEN the blood runs cold and low,
When the winds of doubting blow,
When the shadow of my life
Silences the daily strife,
When the roses fade and fall,
When the violet-odours all
Are sickening with the scent of death,
When the lone soul sorroweth,
What shall light the sombre vale ?
What for comfort shall avail ?

Vague desire and aspiration
Haunt me like an inspiration :

Shadowy hopes that are despairs
Pass and mock my whisper'd prayers :
Solitude, thy silent calm
Lends to me no hallowed balm ;
I am fully mournful only
When most intimately lonely ;
When in the busy haunts that teem
With many a bruit of active scheme,
I crack the jest, and laugh my fill,
My demon laughs as loudly still ;
Yet in the sight of other eyes
He frees me from his sorceries,
And then my weary spirit knows
A little respite of repose :
With Nature, too, a happy time
Is dedicate to thoughtful rhyme,
And in her presence I enjoy
Short solace for my great annoy.

I wander'd down the grassy steep,
Where purple orchis-blossoms sleep,
Waiting until the voice of Spring
Shall wake them into blossoming ;—

E

Alas ! their Spring is yet to come ;
They nestle in a happy home ;
But mine, that such a promise bore,
Is frost-nipp'd and can bloom no more.
Beneath the slope, the fringèd sea,
Lulled by its own low minstrelsy,
Was dreaming in the amber light
Which like a woven mantle bright
The sun threw o'er it.　Here and there
Great gulls flapp'd through the heavy air,
And, on the pebble-girdled shore,
The pale green wavelets o'er and o'er
Went tumbling with a drowsy sense
Of universal indolence.
It was a day as sweet as rare,
When January, cold and bare,
Put on for once the golden hue
Of apple-blossom time.　I grew
Heart-soften'd by the warm excess
Of unexpected loveliness ;
And for a while forgot the shade
That lurks for me in every glade,
The bony fear that will not rest,
Nor pause from troubling my poor breast.

I cannot hope to live again,
And lose this load of quiet pain,
Until the years that speed so fast
Shall bring delightful calm at last !
The grand fulfilment of desire
Shall tip their angel-wings with fire,
Or else the lapse of time shall bless
My spirit with forgetfulness ;
God in his mercy grant me peace,
And bid this demon-sorrow cease,
Or bear me in his arms of love
To amaranthine bowers above !

EUTHANASIA.

I.

THE dim hours come ; I see adown the street
    The few from toil releas'd,
Pass joyous onward, glad, elate, and fleet,
    Unto their evening feast.

II.

Upon the soft sill of this casement high
    My burning cheek is laid,
The while I strive within the golden sky
    To hold the hues that fade.

IIL

Yet duskier now, and, every moment still,
    Gloomier and more dull,
The narrow way beneath with night doth fill,
    With Night the beautiful!

IV.

O Night! that leavest on mine eyelids weak
    The heav'nly sacred balm,
Bring now no more the dreams of what I seek,
    Nor yet bright Victory's palm;

V.

Bind thou sweet Hope; and bid Ambition sink
    Under dark Lethe's stream;
And Self-Reproach drug thou with poppy-drink
    Till even it shall dream.

VI.

Alas! e'en thus, O Night! one eve just fled,
    I supplicated thee.—
Ah, woe is me! that now the lost and dead
    Should nigh forgotten be!

VII.

As now, so hurried forward here below,
  Along the dusty way,
Sweet maids and many a youth towards the flow
  Of Arno to the Bay;

VIII.

And shadows up the tall house gleam'd and died
  Before the sinking sun,
And fire-flies sparkled on the near hill-side
  The hour when work was done;

IX.

The while that star which wakes the sleeping moon,
  And leads her o'er each hill,
Upon the topmost tuft of cypress soon
  Unshifting shone and still.

X.

And on this terrace from afar I caught
  The soft faint mountain line,
Which dared the crowding mists that vainly sought
  To enwrap the Apennine.

XI.

O kingly Hills! with snow-lit brows divine
 And forest-circled throne!
That eve your glory unto me did shine
 Oppressive, white, and lone.

XII.

Oblivion came not with the night, and I
 In wild delirium pray'd
That Love might bind me, or that I might die
 As moon-wrapt cloudlets fade.

XIII.

Oh! many a prayer, or mute, or half-express'd,
 I stammer'd wearily,
Wistfully watching those who pass'd with zest
 To midnight revelry.

XIV.

When lo! unto me came that blessed joy,
 Long pray'd for in my dreams,—
Came like that music which can never cloy,
 The murmur of far streams.

XV.

Beneath me was a step—a rustling heard,—
 I started carelessly,
And saw a Form that all my pulses stirr'd
 Move towards me glimmeringly:

XVI.

The myrtle was uplifted, and a hand
 Upon my arm was press'd,
And then the sweetest voice in that sweet land
 Murmur'd—"Take *now* thy rest;

XVII.

" Tortur'd—abandon'd—thou shalt own no more
 The reign of pain and hate,
But to some dim and unimagin'd shore
 Work out the ways of Fate.

XVIII.

"Vainly thou strivest for forgetfulness
 Of that which once was dear;
Thou shalt, believe me, yet—ay now, confess
 Thy past is not so drear."

XIX.

Thus she, as lifting up her deep dark eyes
 With startling dazzling haste,
I drank her beauty as the faint may-flies
 The river-breathings taste ;

XX.

And sighs, that had been fetter'd many a year
 In frost-bound iron pride,
Arose, and scatter'd every trivial fear,
 As she sank by my side :

XXI.

Whilst, through the grape-hung lattice over us,
 The white moon came and bless'd
With glory her low forehead luminous,—
 With calm the hand I press'd.

XXII.

" The curls around my brow, sweet maid, may speak
 Of youth, at least, to thee ;
Yet that is past, and I can only seek
 A home beyond Life's sea.

LYRICS.

XXIII.

" Yet oh ! that beauty like to thine should gleam
　　Across my burden'd way !
For all thy loveliness hath made my dream
　　A spectral holiday.

XXIV.

" Thou canst awake the past, all cleans'd from gall
　　And unexalting fears;
Breathe gently, Love, upon me, and make fall
　　The unaccustom'd tears!"

XXV.

—Ah! thus I spake: and she with soft words bade
　　My trancèd soul adieu,
And left me murmuring o'er the words she said,
　　With recollection true ;

XXVI.

Words unforgotten;—yet I never can
　　In calm coherence weave
The sinuous threads of subtle speech that then
　　Made mystical that eve.

XXVII.

Vales where the thin streams wander, deep and dim,
    'Neath marble hills of pine
That darkening downward to the water's rim
    Shall hear these plaints of mine,—

XXVIII.

These shall enfold me in their solitude,
    Receive my painless breath,
And thou, blest Spirit, shalt make dumb the rude
    And sudden sound of Death.

XXIX.

And though another quiet midnight may
    Bring momentary peace,
And though one more Italian azure day
    May rise to bid care cease;

XXX.

No more am I with terrors grim and wild
    At fierce undying strife;
For now with Life's dim ways is reconcil'd
    That golden glory—Life!

ODE TO SPRING.

TO A FRIEND.

THOU dost well to sigh for Spring,
For the joys which she doth bring,
For the fresh and blushing morn
When the youthful Hope is born,—
For the even's dying glory,
When the lover tells his story
To his Sweet, if he be glad,
Or, if doubting grown and sad,
To the Moon he lifts his voice
Till she biddeth him rejoice,
While, on all around, the hour
Exercising magic power,
Peace doth reign, supreme and still,
Down the vale and on the hill;—
For the solemn-starrèd nights
And their balmy warm delights,

When throughout the budding grove
Forms there flit all life and love,
Poets' fancies, blithe and bright,
Circled round by mystic light ;—
For the sweet and happy days
Hallow'd by the mellow lays—
Birds' sweet carols—to the breeze
Sent from out the swinging trees,
That, as we enrapt do lie
In long grass up-gazing high,
Come in streams of music gushing,
Smooth and strong, as if no hushing
Bleating lamb or babbling brook,
Shepherd's song or cawing rook,
Ever to their joy could send
Mirth to stay or pleasure end.

'Tis the season when all Love
From beneath us and above
Universally doth burst ;
From the earth, though labour-curs'd,
Springs the evidence sublime,
Spotless from all taint of crime,

White and pure as snowy lily,
Bold and crown'd as daffodilly,
All embracing and all blessing
With her pure and fond caressing;
Love the spirit then revealeth
All the beauty she concealeth,
When the Winter, Death, hides all
Summer's sweetness 'neath his pall;
Like renew'd Delight she springeth
From the clay-cold earth, and wingeth
Through the azure depths that glow
'Twixt pilèd clouds of mountain snow,
Hanging in effulgence clear
Round each night-illuming sphere,
Paving white Diana's path,
Spell-commanding, to the earth,
Whispering from the mountains lone
Tales of bright Endymion;
O'er the wide unresting ocean
Hovering with an easy motion,
Warming all the water's life
Till the waves forget their strife,
While each snowy-pebbled cove,

Growing calm and clear as Love,
Leaving undisturb'd the fair
Waving groves of sea-weed rare,
On its leafy-skirtèd shore
Rolls in sleepy murmur o'er ;
For the Zephyrs are up-bound,
Earthquake sleepeth underground,
Lightning, from the calmèd North,
Pale reflection sendeth forth,
By no thunder loud attended,
Nor with hurtful flashing splendid ;
And Apollo, in new brightness,
Smiling at Love's mirthful lightness,
Looketh from his palace halls,
As his radiancy falls
On the Alpine mountains olden
With a glory warm and golden ;
On the silent buried vallies,
Whence the silver streamlet sallies ;
On the laughing rushing river,
And the plains and dells that quiver
'Neath the softly drooping cloud,
Hiding blessing in a shroud,

Which goes drifting over bowers,
Over towns and over towers,
Borne afar by wingèd showers,
Whose pinions glance within the sun
Through the rack all dense and dun,
Through the white and glistening hail,
And the vaporous misty veil,
O'er the heads of distant mountains,
Gleaming in late-fallen fountains,
Till the blue and beaming heaven,
Undefac'd by murky leaven,
Calmly deep and all intense,
Round the clear-cut edges dense
Of the storm-cloud, darkly shines
Like a twilight over pines.

O thou darling of the Year!
Youth oppos'd to Autumn sere!
Maid belov'd and ever-loving!
With whose pulse the Earth is moving,
As her promise blustering March
On the early-greening larch
On the violet and primrose,

Blithely in his passage throws !
O thou lovely Maid divine !
Whose blue eyes so deeply shine
With the passion fine and clear
Of many an azure-banded sphere,
Passion mystical and strange,
Knowing neither bound nor range,—
Earth with all thy beauty's ringing,
Let us aye thy praise be singing !

Thou Light of Hope ! Thou Guide of Love'
Stooping from thy throne above,
Come in fullest bliss before us,
Follow'd by thy heavenly chorus.
Let but Love, and Love alone,
Lead us where all joys have flown ;
Holding sanctuary in thy breast
From the world's most cruel unrest !
Inspirer thou of Poets' deeming
Wondrous truths in wildest dreaming ;
Cherisher of youngling flowers
Thro' the tender April hours ,
Thou, of Poets, Poet only,

F

Who from the Winter's night most lonely
Dost create all forms of light
New-inform'd with splendour bright!

Ah! thou Spirit brave! who can
Hope thy glories e'er to span,
Measure all thy loving works
Or the power that in them lurks,
Take account of all thy wonders,
Mightier than Jove's fiercest thunders,
And more subtle than the spell
Dian casts o'er Heaven and Hell?
Thou the new Prometheus art,
Who, with bold and single heart,
Deep within the snow-clad Earth
Mov'st unseen, amid the mirth,
Savage-like and foul and drunken,
In which Winter's slaves are sunken;
And, anon! the earth conceiving,
Thou, thro' storms, thy quick way cleaving,
Fliest to the halcyon clime
Of the god that blesseth rhyme;
Thence with music, weird and fated,

All thy heart intoxicated,
Thou returnest, richly freighted,
Bearing on thy lips a fire
Shapèd like Apollo's lyre ;
And thy warm and healing breath
Soon destroys the reign of Death ;
As on pinions, fleet and fair,
Purifying earth and air,
Touching soft the chilly ground,
Whence the lovèd life doth bound,
Whilst thou'rt winging, with sweet singing
All Earth's mighty heart is ringing.

Oh ! well may I now despair
As I think how many fair
Spring-delights we may enjoy,
Ne'er to cumber, nor to cloy,
Which I, being but a mortal,
Have o'erlook'd 'neath Song's fair portal.
Come thou soon, thou golden Prime,
When we make the honey'd rhyme,
Where the maiden's pouting kisses
Are the deepest of all blisses

That in quiet vale we snatch;
While from all around we catch
Wand'ring scents of opening flowers
Greeting all the younger hours
Of the luscious-breasted Summer;
While each yellow-banded hummer,
Busied with his dainty treats,
Gives us thoughts of other sweets;
While the rapture-movèd bird
In the copse is sweetly heard,
And our hearts unto his lay
Move responsive, as we say,
To the Girl we love most dearly,
That which he says not more clearly,
Nor with lighter heart elate,
To his silent trancèd mate!

Love! thou art the light of Spring!
Now thy healing influence bring!
Let us with the ancient earth
Drown past ills in present mirth,
Laughing, quaffing, voices ringing,
While the Earth to Spring is singing!

ODE TO THE EARTH.

I.

O THOU eternal Danae, whose breast
  Is open ever to the showering gold,
  Who ever dost in thy warm arms enfold
The god-like fervour, by a god possess'd !
Now, while the glory of the happy May
  Is robing thee in festal bravery
    Of vernal foliage gay,
And the sweet birds on every leafy spray
  Bright minstrels are, that hymn their love to thee,—
I, too, though less melodious far than they,
  Yet loving thee, O Mother, fervently,
Would sing, though faltering, one impassion'd song
In token of the praises that belong
To thee, who art our goddess, by great Jove
Lov'd, and made worthy of our reverent love.

II.

In every ferny brake and hollow wild,
   Warm'd into life, the children of the spring
   Leap in their glory, and on foot or wing
Go forth through fair green leafage undefil'd ;
   Long shoots of lush and thornless eglantine
      Fill up the darkening ways,
Through which Apollo darts his arrowy rays
   From rosy morn on till his slow decline ;
Now Philomel trills out her tenderest lays
In fragrant valleys when the moon is low ;
   And listening ye may hear, when she is dumb,
The sweet sedge-warbler, ere the night-winds blow,
   Piping a feebler treble, till there come
Faint echoes from the hollow elms a-row.

III.

Mother, the skies that o'er thy flowery dells
   Bend as a solemn dome, are calm and blue ;
   Now floats a white cloud-island slowly through
The stainless realms where nothing evil dwells ;
   And like a bird on spirit-wings I rise
Far up to its pure cliffs, and thence gaze down

On all thy beauty with enamoured eyes ;
For Loveliness is on thy brows a crown,
    And, in the clear sunlighted weather,
      Glory and Hope and Love seem met together,
To fill the air with dreams of Paradise,
    And that first mystic day,
    When out of Chaos and dim Night God drew
Thy glimmering orb, and sped thee on thy way !

IV.

Then, waking from that strange primeval trance,
    With joy thou didst His guiding voice obey,
And watched the planets in their pearly dance
    Attend thy motion in a proud array ;
Then o'er thy caverns and thy gleaming vales
    Flew the clear-wingèd Spirit of the Spring,
      And in her hands did bring
Such wealth of life, whether of leaf or limb,
    That even the glad revival of to-day,
      The fresh young breath that hails
The music of this morn, were all too dim
    To shadow forth the least of that delight,
    When every gloomy corner was made bright

With flushing wings, with blithesome feet that
    glance,
And all the green-wood joy of earliest May.

v.

How to the core was thy profound heart stirr'd
    By all this light, and fair tranquillity '
Yet from the heavens came down one awful word;
    And how was all thy splendour gone and fled,—
        Gone like the spirit of one dead !
    For o'er thy breast flow'd the remorseless sea;
The long roll of the stormy waves was heard
In each green valley, where the brooding bird,
Deep in the noiseless leafage, had found rest,
        And a fair sylvan nest;
    The voice of many waters only sounded
Through the abyss, where still thy darkling globe
    Roll'd on its ceaseless course, for ever bounded
By the dim belt of floods as by a robe.

VI.

Then o'er thy weltering rim one moment hover'd
    An angel, fire-envelop'd, rainbow-wing'd,

And with a rod smote the long wave that cover'd
    Thy aching orb; the abyss was ring'd
With flame that lit thy sad and gloomy path,
    And lick'd the waters with its arrowy heat;
      The glory that then pulse-like beat
Upon the waters, dried their might away.
Ah! even in this repose which thy heart hath
    In these late times, thou canst recall that day
      Of comfort after anguish, the defeat
Of adverse powers that marr'd thy early love,
And the victorious aid that hail'd thee from above!

VII.

The island-cloud whereon my spirit sate
    Has faded like white foam upon the shore;
    For a swift wind its gauzy fabric tore:
      And now on viewless wings elate
      I speed my visionary flight
O'er bosky glen, and heather-mantled height;
    Be thou my Guide, my Teacher, and inspire
      My heart with such poetic fire,
    That ever where my else-unheeded voice
Shall echo through the land, all men may know

That I have been with thee, and may rejoice,
And feel their weary hearts with hope and gladness
　　glow.

VIII.

Far in warm lands across the Atlantic sea
　　Hast thou no home, O Mother, for thy child,
　　Where in the southern forest, dim and wild,
I might hold sweet communion silently
With all thy fairest subjects, and with thee?
　　There, there, where thou art queen and uncontroll'd,
　　Where gentle creatures still are calm and bold,
Where troops of mild-eyed deer unharass'd graze,
　　Might I not walk, and with down-gazing eyes,
　　Ponder in silence, and grow pure and wise,
　　　Till, led by thee, and full of Magian lore,
I might return, and teach in tuneful lays
　　　The lessons of those quiet days;
　　Or else, in that fair wilderness grown old,
Lay on thy kindly breast my scanty locks and hoar?

IX.

Silence, weak heart! no words of thy repining
　　Can change the order of the fateful years;

Gaze rather at the wreath the Hours are twining
  In this chill northern land ! the time for tears
Is fled, with all the sorrows of the snow :
Now once again the milder zephyrs blow ;
  Flower-buds are dreaming in the deep fresh grass ;
Waken, O Earth, my dull and weary spirit,
          New glory to inherit !
Teach these faint eyes what sacred pleasures flow
From thy least valued places ; wherefore go
  To distant lands, when beauties here surpass
    All that a poet in his dreams can see ?
Therefore with humbled heart and head bent low,
    Here will I rest until thou speak'st to me !

                    x.

Great Mother, now thy solemn voice I hear !
  Forgive the lightness of my opening song,
  In which I did thy serious story wrong,
With idle names of worship old and sere,
Prating to thee of Grecian gods once dear
  To priest and poet ! empty dreamers they !
The gods they dreamt of, all are pass'd and dead !
Rather would I with bow'd, uncover'd head,

Alone with thee, a juster tribute pay,
 With reverent voice, to Him who set thee here ;
  Who guides thee on thy wild mysterious way ;
 Whose power and love surpass all earthly measure ;
  Who clothes thee now with all the bloom of May,
 And fills thy vales with green and golden treasure,
And decks thy mountain-sides with purple hues of
  pleasure !

ODE ON THE DEATH OF THOMAS CHATTERTON.

AUGUST 24, 1770.

i.

List, list, O placid stream! and thou fair maid,
   Sabrina! rise from out thy root-bound cell,
And with thy cool white fingers swift unbraid
   Thy goldy locks, entangled in some dell,—
   Some rushy dell wherein the amorous pray'r
   Of river sprite detains thee! Oh! repair,
Cleaving the light-green ripple, undisguised
   Unto my yearning soul! Loosen in me,
To all the unhearing winds and pastures mute,
   My song imprison'd, lowly, and unpriz'd!
   I bend me to thy wave : my longings flee

Unutter'd o'er thy breast, as if to suit
Thy mood of deep repose, thy spirit's airless lute!

II.

Waken, oh! waken, from thy pensive dreaming!
    With me, O maiden'! 'twixt broad swan-wings
      glide,
My hastening thoughts upon thy flow are streaming
    To where Bristowa lifts her head of pride :
    There shall thy plaintive pipings me inspire
    To strike in sadness my unlaurell'd lyre ;
There 'neath the steep of Clifton's lofty plain,
    Our winged bark shall steer her solemn way,
A thing of whiteness strange amid the night ;
    And our wild hymning then, no longer twain,
    Shall blend in Song, as dusk and dawn in day,
Striking the hoary City with affright,
As olden masquers risen with weird disguisement dight.

III.

Ah! woe is me for dread!   Ah! cold the night
    Stoopeth across these level twilight meadows ;
No guardian nymph, with eyes all glowworm-bright,
    Breaketh the wave beneath the alder shadows ;

Dead, dead thou art, and dark, O chilly stream!—
The idle mirror of my idle dream;
Can Chatterton then die, and Earth, asleep,
Await the coming morn in dull repose?
Thy waves, O Avon! say, can they move on
Unheeding hearts that bleed and eyes that
weep?
Alas! thy unawaken'd being flows
Beneath eve's low-hung star without one moan
For him whose love thou wast, whose sprite's for ever
flown!

IV.

O whence, dear Mother, whence, O Earth, dost thou
This web of chill indifference weave round
Thy old, thy passion-fretted breast, that now
Sorrow should steep thee in a peace profound?
Ah! whence thy calm?—for fair, oh! fair, was he
Whose passing hath so much absorb'd from thee!
—Light from thy skies hath flown, and night appears
Haggard and restless 'neath the shapeless moon;
And all thy shades and hues distorted are,
In scenes that once awaken'd painless tears,
Where Love oft pin'd and, pining, gain'd the boon

Long wept and sought for.   Oh ! that theme so fair
Should mock my tortur'd soul and, maddening, urg'
   despair !

v.

When Chatterton's proud being clove the air,
   And touch'd thy breast, O Earth, a tongue of flame,
Too much his soul with ardour, fierce and fair,
   Endowèd was ; thus him thou dost reclaim
   Back to thy ancient bosom ere the spark
   Kindled a world, and lit the eternal Dark
With awful breathings in the vast Inane !
   Thus Fiends—ah ! could we Mercies call them !—
     drove
The heaven-born soul from woe to biting woe ;
   Insult with gibing, Want and Grief with pain,
   And Disappointment tediously strove
To force their captive his last ghastly foe
To embrace with sharp despair, and front Death's sudden
   flow.

VI.

O Earth ! perchance thou'rt glad ; and, in deep joy,
   No sympathetic thrillings from thy core
Dost thou send forth, to pay the world's annoy,

Fraught with the mystery of thy ancient lore;
And lo! that soul of flame, that ruddy star
That flash'd, portending strife and storm and war,
Amid the awaken'd gloom a blinding light
To unregenerate minds and selfish slaves,
Now hath accomplish'd his brief mission here;
And stricken-through, he, blinded in the night,
Fell death-cold to a place of many graves,
Where Horror, hung with marsh lights, by his bier
Gloom'd o'er his tender limbs, and blanch'd those lips
so dear!

VII.

I had a vision in the stormy night;—
Rouse thee, O City!—and thou western river!
Stay thy cold flow, and 'neath the pale moonlight
Let my sad story freeze thy restless quiver!
Alas! that ye, cold spires, alone should be
The careless bearers of my plaint to sea!—
Still may thy sounding bells with long-drawn wail
Raise sweet response to this my hymn of woe,
And o'er the Atlantic wave to lands afar
Bear the lone echo of this solemn tale,

And make the Stranger's tear indignant flow ;
For here men's sleeping souls indifferent are,
Or big with hopeful scheme, or bow'd in earthly
    care !

VIII.

Oh ! what a sickness on my spirit fell,
    When first thy fate, sweet soul, drank up my
        hearing !
Each ghastly detail, like a blast from hell,
    All faith and hope destroy'd, with terror searing ;
    And through the blank of one most tedious night
    I wander'd, haunting all the Avonian height,
And, in a stupor, nor alive nor dead,
    Musing upon the terrac'd town that lay
Dark in the dense obscure beneath me spread,
    Light bore me through a wilderness of time,
        Light, that meeting light, did merge
           Into eternal day !
And, borne above the mazy baffling surge
    Of interweaving Dreams, o'er heights sublime,
The passage fair, through all the coming years,
        Of thy exalted fame,

With alternating rush of hopes and fears
       Afar I traced,
Mine eyes invisibly upheld and strengthen'd :
       An aye-increasing flame
  That compass'd all, and all things interlaced
      In its far-spreading glow,
So shone, as dim and fair the prospect lengthen'd,
      Which the new years did bring,
The strength matured of Chatterton's renown !
      Far, far beyond the flow
Of years oncoming, in a land of calm,
       Some rose to sing,—
Lifting the while his reputation's crown,—
And sang, in accents sweet as soothing balm,
    How, 'neath the ethereal skies
    O'er which the curtain of the Future lies,
  The minds of men receivèd with delight
The bright-eyed Child of Song, the Bard of Eld ;
    And, lingering long in bitterness and grief
      Upon that awful night
Of horror and despondence and affright,
    One lifted high this song of sweet relief
That all men's troubled hearts with magic held :—

IX.

"O gifted Boy ! no pauper's grave is thine,
　　Nor did thy spirit on the dull earth linger ;
Thy glad young soul across the western brine
　　Flew, pointed homeward by Hope's rosy finger ;
　　The foam-swept billows buoyantly did play
　　Around thy supple limbs and happy way,
And lo ! a sunset, burning in the gold
　　That faerily alit the purple sea,
Found thee upon Atlantis, mystic isle !
　　A new-born spirit of a life untold,
　　In whose harmonious soul all thoughts agree ;
And there new essences of life beguile
Thy curious mind for aye with Love, or Fancy's wile.

X.

"And when that happy isle thy light foot press'd,
　　O joy unutterable and bliss unmeasur'd !—
Fair Forms all rosy-warm thee met with zest,
　　Revealing to thy soul all Beauty treasur'd ;
　　Whilst smiling Peace within the sleeping air
　　And sweet Content embracèd were ;
And from th' eternal trees that swept the sward

The fruits of Glory and of Fame fell down
Upon thy lips to leave a luscious thrill,
  Upon thy locks to trace a lasting crown;
    And thy most rich reward—
Obscuring all Life's recollected ill—
Shall bear ten thousand shapes, all moulded by thy
    will."

XI.

So to my warmèd fancy that bright vision
  With Hope's fond sketch in peace did sweetly
    blend;
Alas! that picture, perfect and Elysian,
  Should bless his after-fame, and not his end!
  Ah! woe for thee, thou boundless soul of pride,
  Cast on the world, wayless and waste and wide,
Oh! how my heart bleeds at thy tale of woe!
  Poor Child of Misery, thou wouldst not bow!—
Thy dauntless soul went forth to meet the days
  Bitter with wretchedness, and on did go,
  Courting To-morrow though despairing *now:*
Till in the mockery of plenteous praise
Thy weary spirit went the worst of darken'd ways!

XII.

When first thy childish hand swept o'er the strings
    Of thy quaint lyre,—that mediæval might,—
Stirr'd were old Bards, as Song forgotten brings
    Eftsoons swift recollection in the night;
    And in their dim and unassailèd home
    Vibrated strongly all the unfathom'd dome
Of cerule air that clasp'd their happiness;
    Enchainèd by the golden-netted wile
    Of thy most subtle smile,
Old Chaucer roused him from the letter'd stone.
       Him did thy vernal chaunt
       Thrill in that grand old haunt,
Where he was lain in peace in time foregone:
    —With what a cheerfulness
He plac'd upon thee bright Apollo's crown!—
       And thou, glad soul, with rapture failing,
       Whilst poets all thy youth were hailing,
Catching, anon, thy master's eye
Pierc'd with thy eagle sight the distant blue,
And with the ocean, Song, as on a rocky shore,
Burst forth tumultuous, rolling o'er and o'er,
Borne on the light and dazzling spray on high;

And now thy full heart to the heavens flew
And floated airily 'mid sunny isles ;
And then, swift sweeping thro' the thunderous piles
  Of lurid cloud-forms,
  Thy spirit fell adown the clashing storms
   With wild hair streaming,
   And glar'd—a red lightning flash !
O Soul of passion ! like a sudden clash,
  Dissonant and troublous in my fitful dreaming
   Thy ode swept on, ·
  Whilst o'er each minstrel's head
Keen Inspiration flash'd with hair a-flame !
  And Lydgate, Chaucer's son,
  And Occleve, at the same rare fountain fed,
  And others of unmeasur'd fame,
  And many more of unremember'd name,
Rais'd a glad hymn, lifting thy triumph high :—
  Thou Reader of the Past,
  For aye thy fame shall last,
Till Chaucer's light be blotted from the sky !

XIII.

My vision broke and fled—I know not whither.
  But ah! how harshly day return'd to me;
For then, imprinted deep, as if for ever,
    The suicide's fell purpose seem'd to me
    Ghastly in lineaments, deep-wrought
    In all men's minds by Custom led and taught;
And in the peopled city Love lay chain'd,
    And Execration occupied the seat
Of banish'd Justice in the Council-hall;
    Some were there, who a pitying feeling feign'd,
    More awful far than hatred's open heat;
But through thy native city thy sad fall,
O peerless poet! rais'd the rancorous speech of all.

XIV.

Peace, peace, my heart! Alas! how should they
    know
    The worth they censur'd or the soul they scorn'd?
Dull hearts are they, whose spirits' turgid flow,
    Surcharg'd with grossness, never nobly burn'd;
    In Trade's most level ways for ever bound,
    How could Enthusiasm, inly-crown'd,

Touch their vulgarity with higher light,
    Their calculating brows with verdure wreathe?
Ah! bitter words thou spak'st, words sharp with
      scorn,
    Thee, Chatterton, whose lifted hand did smite,
    Heavy with satires, blasting where they breathe,
Which of thy fellows' failings basely born
Blear'd the pure promise of thy happy April morn.

XV.

Sink not, my heart!   Bear with the mighty thought
    That Chatterton's fair fame was quenchèd never.
The re-informèd Past in splendour wrought
    Glows on his page and speaks of him for ever,
    And now are past for aye the searching pang
    Of cruel Want, and Famine's heedless fang;
The drainèd poison-cup is powerless now,
    To urge his agoniz'd and storm-swept soul.
Yet, oh! for all the hollowness of creed
    That soothèd not his poor tormented brow,
    Nor with sweet after-thoughts could ere condole
With his sad mother in her bitter need,
But, standing coldly by, could e'en approve the deed!

XVI.

Bristowa yet may lift her shameful head,
 And penance do with reverent tone and low,
In that grand Minster of the stone-wrapt dead,
 Melodious with the thought of long ago.
 There Commerce, once thy Genius proud,
 O western City! shall in dust be bow'd,
And Chatterton shall be thy noble theme,
 Thy glory and thy shame, thy high renown,
A warning voice from out the new-born Past,
 A trumpet-sounding from the land of Dream!
 Him shalt thou crown,
Through whose high name thy own shall ever last,
Whose lifted pleading hands thou from thy sight didst
 cast!

XVII.

Peace, peace!—once more I breathe the sacred air,
 The dwelling-place of ever-brooding peace,
That in this dim long aisle of beauty rare
 Calms the hot pulse and bids Life's fever cease;
 O thou grand pile!—of ancient thought
 The resurrection-life, with vigour fraught,
If thou must fall, in Chatterton's fair name

I pray that pastoral calm alone may fan
Thy hoary desolation with sweet airs.
O may thy end, unmarr'd by sword and flame,
Be calm and sweet and euthanasian,
That Time, whose arm, nor Power nor Grandeur
spares,
May be by Love unnerv'd when he thy beauty dares!

XVIII.

Then sing, O ancient City!—let thy lays
Bid Calumny her work for ever cease;
The charity of brighter, better days,
Thy hallow'd fane shall gild with new-born peace:
And aye unto thy shrine
The bond that is divine
Shall draw pale pilgrims from the world's far lands
To taste the quiet springs of pure repose.
So shall the old Red Cliffe exalted be,
Crown'd by that grey antiquity which stands,
Like kingly Lear, white with a thousand woes,
Bare to the senseless storms' unfeeling glee,
O'er-arching in deep gloom a matchless memory!

THE TOMB IN THE GARDEN.

"In the Garden a new Sepulchre."

PH OF ABIMATHEA *and others enter, bearing the body of* JESUS, *and singing.*

SWEET Silence reigns in this calm place
With more than all her wonted grace ;
The cassia wastes its deep perfume
In breezes that the sands consume ;
And with their hues the bright flowers bless
The all-surrounding wilderness.

The only sound in all the dell
Is the bluff bee in the lily-bell :

He shakes the golden dust around
The scarlet petals' stately bound,
And sings as loud as sing he can,
Secure from greed of thieving man.

The long, long shadows on the grass
Still lengthen as the slow hours pass :
A sultry twilight follows soon
On the hot and noiseless afternoon:
And to this garden still and fair
Our cold and lifeless Lord we bear.

See on the whiteness of his brow
The ruddy blood crept trickling slow ;
The thorny crown has riv'n the fair
And rolling waves of his bright hair ;
Close with a touching of thy lips
Those blue eyes darken'd in eclipse !

And now while fast the warm tears flow
Upon the chilly face below,
We lay the treasure of all time,
The theme of angel-poets' rhyme,

Within the marble tomb, hard by
The garden blooming ceaselessly.

Still shall the morning sun illume
The sweet flowers round this quiet tomb :
Still shall the heedless bee sing o'er
The lilies that he priz'd before ·
But He that made the whole world bright,
Has left it for the realms of night !

As they depart, a SERAPH *is discovered in the tomb, supporting*
the head of the SAVIOUR. *To him a* CHERUB —

CH. Launching from the clear radiance of a star,
I heard thy sad voice, calling from afar :
More swift than lightning through the vast of space
I come into the sunshine of thy face.

SER. Behold the beauty, mark the silent spell,
That in these pale and deathly features dwell !
Hold up the body ! 'Tis a joy to bear
The earthly covering of a soul so fair !

H

CH. Who is he ?   My thoughts are folden
        In the calm eyes cold before us ;
    Through his hair run lights more golden
        Than the orb suspended o'er us !

SER.   Follow me in solemn chorus.

[*Sings.*

        Hail, O loving eyes and holy,
        Tearful aye, and melancholy !
        Hail, fair brow, so sadly torn
        By the wreath of human scorn !
        Oh ! forgive that crown of thorn !

                CHORUS.

        Pardon all the human scorn.

        Hail, sweet hands, too waxy-white,
        Save where Roman nails did smite !
        Dear dead fingers, that have bless'd
        Little children, and caress'd
        Babes upon the mother's breast !

CHORUS.

Now for ever laid to rest.

Hail, dear mouth, so foully smit,
By the men that heard from it
Only words of love and pity,
Even in the doomèd city!
Pardon, Lord, the blinded city!

CH. (*perplexedly*).

Stay the fervour of thy singing,
    For thy words of song thrill through me,
And thy last strange speech is ringing
    Through my pulse, till thou renew me
    With a reassurance to me!

SER. Wait, and in silent weeping ease thy heart!

[*Sings.*

Lingering long, and loath to move,
Yearn'd thy all-forgiving love:
But the Father's time was come,
When to his supernal home
We might welcome once again,
Our adored——

H 2

CH. "Might welcome home!" but we for ever part
With human souls upon the grave's sad brink!

SER. Yet shall this human soul for ever drink
Delicious draughts of immortality.

CH. Ah! Seraph, say, how can this wonder be?
Great Enoch, when the sea-less earth he trod,
And, being pure in spirit, walk'd with God,
One morning, when the cold grey peaks were crown'd
With golden air of sunrise, was not found.
Elijah too, who, upright and austere,
Walk'd through the nations with a godly fear,
'Midst acclamations from each hymning choir,
Was drawn to heaven by wingèd steeds of fire.
These blessed men, through grace of God most high,
Received the favour that they should not die:
But this fair mortal has already gone
To silent shores where never light hath shone.

SER. Then know that this is the Almighty Son;
Th' Eternal Word; who, with the Father one,
Throughout the hoary past eternity

Was crown'd with all the awful joys that be
Concentred in that universal sway,
That knows no rise, no summit, no decay.

CH. And is this He ! humbly on bended knee
To his dead shell I bow adoringly.
                              [*After a paus*.

  I know it all, the woe, the shame,
  The scorn heap'd on the lowly name
  He honour'd when to earth He came.

  I see the hungry faces there ;
  The agony of silent prayer ;
  The pain and laughter sore to bear.

  Brother, a change comes o'er thy face,
  And o'er thy locks a lambent grace,
  Like far light from a holy place.

SER. Into the dark I seem to raise
  Prophetic vision, and to gaze
  On actions of the future days.

CH. What happiness is hidden there !

O say, what rais'd the weight of care,
And made thy sad brow clear and fair?

SER. I see a little room apart ;
Few sit there, dull and sad at heart.

CH. Why should that dismal sight renew
Thy lifted eyes with living blue ?

SER. The room is shaken where they sit ;
God's fiery Spirit visits it,
And saith, "O ye of little wit,
Ye love the dead one ; and ye know
He is not dead, but living so
That He can hear you pray below !
Be glad then !   Fill with sacred force
The world, as rain-floods at the source
Fill up an arid watercourse ! "

CH. Ah ! brother, then the glow of light,
That glorified thy face with might,
Came reflex from their inner sight !

[*Here they sit silent a while*

CH. Seraph, the light has faded from thine eyes;
And all the changing tints of rainbow dyes,
That gave thy crimson wings fresh loveliness,
Have fail'd; and in thy features new distress
Arises like a pale moon wrapp'd in mist.

SER. Saw'st thou the shadowy form that came and
      kiss'd
The dead brow that was his?

CH.   I only gazed
Into the stillness of thy deep eyes raised
To heaven for consolation, and my ears
Listen'd for no sound but thy falling tears.

SER. It was the desolate Jerusalem!
She who for aye has madly murder'd them
Who lov'd her; and the One who lov'd her best
She thrust most rudely from her maniac breast.

CH. Has she no hope? Cannot this kiss atone?

SER. I gaze into the future, but her moan
Drowns the response. Ay me! while yet He trod

The barren hills, lorn of the smile of God,
It would have brought into an angel's eyes
(Could angels weep for mortal miseries)
The bitter tears, to see how men withstood
The unselfish love He sealèd with his blood.

   CH. E'en as thou speakest, to my wond'ring mind
A doubt comes swifter than the wingèd wind.
Say, taking pity on my feebler sense,
Did any subtle and dim influence
Move in the gusty halls of heaven, when He
Walked this low earth ?   Or tell me, didst thou see
A fluttering movement of the planet-cars,
A darkening tumult in the pearly stars,
A sickening faintness in the pulse of air ?
Or, were thine eyes, ineffable and fair,
Made capable to watch from that high throne
The Lord of glory, with all glory gone ?

   SER. Cherub, by right we hold a higher place,
And nearer station to the Holy Face,
Than ye, whose throbbing choirs of purest blue
Circle around us in attendance due.
Ye, gazing ever towards the source of light,

See but our splendour and the vault of night :
We, from a height sublimer, more august,
Can watch the actions of the breathing dust,
And clear below, though narrow'd to a span,
Behold the motions of poor mortal Man.
Of late the view—at all times worthy note,
Since first God made in dusky ether float
The sun-illumin'd globe—most strange has been,
Since One has with his presence made serene
The warring winds, and wrought upon the sea
Quick halcyon charms of perfect potency.
Learn then that I have watch'd this Man divine
Since first He deign'd to claim the royal line
Of Judah's David : all our flaming host,
Star-crown'd, and bearing, in the innermost
Recesses of our being, glowing fires,
Outward-refulgent, with our sacred lyres
For ever strung to chant Jehovah's praise,—
We, in this glory, hush'd our tuneful lays,
And silence reign'd in Heaven.

CH.   We still sang on ;
Our faint, sweet voices rang in unison,

As round and round the splendour of your ranks,
Ye warriors of the Lord in proud phalanx,
We, gentler spirits, wheel'd in love and awe,
Still singing, but more faintly, as we saw
Your mighty harps had ceas'd the thrill that sent
Loud melody to all the winds.   What lent
That sudden silence to your minstrelsy
We knew not.

SER.   'Twas the King of all, 'twas He !
A little child in pastoral meanness laid
Among the senseless brutes that low'd and bray'd,
Unseen of men, unthought of, and unlov'd,
That Babe with such an awe our cohorts mov'd,
That angels in mute adoration bow'd,
Who reign in glory, loftiest of the proud.
In that great silence, and with looks so bent,
We gaz'd upon the growing child, still pent
In household bonds of mothers' maxims fine,
And petty dogmas ruling the Divine.

CH. Could not the love of all our starry powers
Comfort the sadness of those cheerless hours?

Could not his spirit, hungering patiently,
Be fed with solace from his home on high?
And through the toil of all his earthly way
Some angel bear the languor of a day?

SER. Yea, once! We watch'd Him with the same
    intense
Deep silence, through his childhood's innocence,
And boyhood's years, while dimly through the screen
Of human flesh shone out the light serene.
At last when, grown a man, he pass'd his days
In quiet labour, full of gentle grace,
The mortal still with power to render null
The grand immortal,—till the time was full;
Then suddenly we watch'd him leave behind
The palmy valleys and the fresh hill-wind,
And through the waste and flaring wilderness
With aching footsteps ever onward press.
At last, where all the rocks are bare and white,
And from dark crannies struggle to the light
Black thorny bushes, sapless, cheerless, dead,—
Mocking the sight with forms rememberèd
Of leafy shrub and sweet lush greenery,

So made the saddest thing that man can see,—
His faltering steps the heavenly pilgrim stay'd,
And on a glittering slab his faint limbs laid.
In this sad glen, hemm'd in by boulders rude,
In such a loveless and dull solitude,
A sulphurous cloud, like the envenom'd birth
Of sultry marshes, rose out of the earth,
And as the mists of morning intervene
Between the world and dawn, hid the ravine,
Nor could we see him more.   Day after day,
Sadder, yet silent, where the fog still lay,
We gaz'd in vain, till, after forty times
The sun had roll'd up from the under-climes,
The word of God came unto me; I flew
To meet the mandate with submission due,
And soon my swift obsequious pinions furl'd
Above that silent limit of the world.
The cloud was gone, once more the happy light
Shone brilliant on those cliffs of polish'd white:
E'en as I came, the Arch-fiend Satan rose
With hissing noise, and writh'd in mighty throes:
Shapeless and horrible and huge, he flapp'd
What seem'd his wings; and, in a gloom enwrapp'd,

Fled, moaning, to that dim antarctic cave,
Where round the pole his spectral banners wave,
Where rally in a hideous dance of death
All forms engender'd by his flaming breath.
He, rushing homeward with a hellish cry,
Stain'd with his shadow all the western sky :
But, in the glen, victorious though faint,
The holy Warrior, tried, yet without taint,
Lay as if dying ; I, with helping hand,
Rais'd him, and led him gently through the land,
To where, hard by, a gushing streamlet fell
Adown the rocks into a quiet dell,
And from the windings of its reedy bed
A grateful verdure through the valley spread.
Here in the coolness of the long, sweet grass,
In deepest shadow of the high-cliff'd pass,
I laid him, while the murmur of the bees
Answer'd a whisper in the leafy trees.
The golden kingcups open'd as he came ;
His presence broke their buds to living flame ;
Pure lilies from his footprints sprang, and I
Plucked one and bear it still memorially.
Then drinking of the river, clear and cold,

And, feasting on fresh manna's honey'd gold,
That rain'd upon us from the upper air,
He swiftly gain'd new life and vigour there.
But say, O Cherub, why this altered guise,
And quivering of curv'd lips and downcast eyes?

   Ch. At first, my brother, with admiring thought,
I envied thee the joy that service brought;
And felt a keen pang of now vain desire
That I could then have left the singing choir,
And in humility and menial ways
Have offer'd to our Lord my love and praise.
I envied thee, but, ere the tale was done,
A swift remembrance through my brain did run,
And thy great mission seem'd a little thing !

   Ser. What was this sudden memory that did sting
Thy heart to such a change ?

   Ch.   It was the flower,
The lily-stem, which, on that solemn hour,
Thy hand had pluck'd, that bore the thought to me,
And on my brow wrote such strange charact'ry ;
For, half-forgotten in the lapse of years,

Another lily through the darkness peers,
Borne by seraphic fingers.   Let me tell
Thy courteous patience of this miracle.
I, sailing round the ether of a star,
Bound on some heavenly mission thence afar,
Saw far beneath me, most sublimely winging,
A fiery spirit, who with speed and singing
Mounted the air that kindled as he came ;
Soon at my side his webs of crimson flame
He furl'd, and with a greeting full of grace
Hover'd beside me in that silent place ;
Before his breast he held a lily tall
Whose flowers were purest white, save where did fall
Faint rose reflection from his shadowing wings ;
And still he brooded with low murmurings
Over the stainless petals, and did press
Them to his lips with ardent tenderness.
Soon to my wondering ears he did unfold
The strangest story angel ever told !
Great was the grace, but ah ! my clouded brain
Made all that rare narration void and vain ;
For, till this hour, I never knew aright
The mysteries which thy kindness has made bright.

It seems, that day, he, sent by God Most High,
Had sought a maiden of mortality,
To say that she, a virgin undefil'd,
Should be the mother of a wondrous Child.
He found her in a garden wall'd and sure,
Fit emblem of her sweet life, calm and pure;
And in a vase before her door were set
Three lilies with the morning dew still wet.
His mission over, while the sudden news
Still did her cheeks with mantling flush diffuse,
He rose again to heaven, but bore away
One fragrant token of that solemn day.
No longer I must ponder this in vain,
The child was He who in this tomb is lain!

    SER. But hark! what sound comes through the silent
        air?
What men are these with foreheads bow'd and bare?
Surely this little troop was wont to follow
Christ's sacred footsteps over hill and hollow,
And, with more love than knowledge, faith than wit,
Humbly, as listeners, round his feet to sit.

Down the hill, and by the garden, the DISCIPLES *slowly pass,*
singing :—

Why should we weep and sorrow thus in vain?
    Let us go back again
To those fair shores on which the wavelets break
    Of Galilee's calm lake ;
Once more the nets, once more the little boat,
    Once more again to float
Across the silent water-ways that bore
    Him we shall see no more.

Why did we ever leave those noiseless places,
    To look on busy faces?
We will go back to our old trade again,
    Nor fish for souls of men.
Ay me ! He had a winning voice, and ways
    Full of all love and grace !
None ever spoke such words as this Man said,
    And lo ! this Man is dead !

O thou rock-bulwark'd and imperial town,
    Set on the high hill's crown!
Thou seem'st a lamp lit by pure seraphim,
    Yet art a fen-fire dim !

I

O cruel city, blinded and undone!
   This was the Spotless One :
This was the Man gentle and without stain,
   Who now lies foully slain !

If ye must murder, was there then no death,
   To take away his breath,
Less shameful than this doom of thief and slave ?
   Than this dishonour'd grave?
Ah ! we are simple folk, and cannot know
   The reason of each blow;
We see full little, yet to our poor eyes
   This is not just or wise.

Now all the wishes of our lives are dead,
   With this thorn-crownèd head ;
If anything could cheer our sad hearts yet,
   It would be, to forget !
O calm, cold eyes, and sweet and silent mouth,
   Parched with a deadly drouth !
O sacred Master, whom we lov'd so well !
   For evermore, farewell !

As they depart, SALOME *and* MARY MAGDALENE *timidl approach.*

M. M. Now these are gone, Salome, let us see
Where they have laid Him !

SAL.   Can it, can it be,
That Jesus, lovely Master, lies alone,
Beneath the pressure of that great white stone ?

M. M. My heart is there ! I feel the bitter weight
Oh ! hold my hands till this sharp grief abate '
Salome, I could kill myself for sorrow :
The dismal night-time has a darker morrow.
Each day brings fresh despair ; I feel within,
What brought this woe upon Him was my sin ;
And Hope is gone for ever.

SAL.   Joy is gone,
But Hope, dear sister, kneeling at God's throne,
May not be thrust away. Hope is a lute
That gives sweet songs out, when the birds are
    mute,
In wintry weather. Though the Lord is dead,
Are not His words to be remembered ?

I 2

Did He not say, "Whatever ye may want,
Ask of the Father, He will surely grant"?

M. M. But He is dead! before his living feet
We might pour out our sorrow, might intreat
With weeping eyes and passionate confession,
His gracious pardon and great intercession ;
But who shall go down to the gates of Night,
And through those portals find his way aright,
Question the gibbering ghosts and flitting shades
Whether his shadow yet their calm invades ?
And, having found him, should a man embrace
Feet of a spirit, or a phantom face?
There sit the Kings, and He, a King, will take
His throne there in a silence none may break.

SAL. But God,—our Father, as we learn'd to
     say,
By listening to his doctrine day by day,—
God is not dead : the earthly help may be
Remov'd, to clear dim eyes that will not see !
The glittering lines of morning mist are bright

With gold and purple gleams of tender light ;
Their fairness tempts the eye to wish their stay,
And blame the beams that clear their veil away ;
But when the sun has burst that cloudy prison,
And on the world in fullest glory risen,
Charm'd by his splendour, we no more regret
The loss that brought that blessing.

M. M.　　　　　　　　　　　　　Eyes are wet
In this wild world of sorrow for all woes,
Yet every mortal grief claims some repose
In lapse of time ; but this despair of mine
Must be unchanging as the hopes divine
That were its source of being.　Years may roll
Their deadening circles o'er my weary soul,
But respite from this aching weight of sin,
Nor prayer, nor patient suffering e'er can win !

SAL. I still would hope !　But if no other plea
Can wean you from this wailing misery,
Look up at least, and to your heart confess
This woman knows a deeper wretchedness !

M. M. Mary! his mother! let us go, nor pain
Her broken heart with our distress in vain.

As they hurry away, the MOTHER *of* JESUS *comes near, and
throws herself down before the Tomb. After a silent interval
she says —*

Weep, Mothers of Jerusalem ! and ye
   Who through the ages wail for children dead,
Rise from your stony tombs and mourn with me,
   With me, whose grief is so divinely fed
   With blighted hopes and dreams that round his
     head
Wove their delightful garlands ; rise and say
   " Our wretched hearts with bitter sorrow
But she is cast upon a sadder way,
Is rack'd by fiercer woes, shrinks from more blank
    dismay !

  " We wept to soothe a mother's natural love,
   And sigh'd to lose the long desire of years ;
A few near friends whom our wild grief did move
   Bow'd o'er the grave and mingled quiet tears ;
   The world knew nothing of our hopes and fears ;

But on this woman " (ye shall say) "there lies
    The utter weight of such despair as seres
A man, who sees with swift prophetic eyes,
A scheme to save the world, and hears the world
    despise ! "

Go back to those dim haunts of silentness,
    From which my fancy called you ! Shades of
       night !
I once might dream to see your footsteps press
    These well-known precincts in the happy light !
    Sweet legendary matrons, fairly dight
In spotless robes of purest chastity !
    Are you for ever crush'd by death's chill blight?
Is there no second life, where piety
Shall meet its lov'd and lost, and ne'er more parted
    be?

The lips that taught me such a happy creed
    Are silent, and the eyes of heavenly blue,
In whose divinest depths my heart could read
    More love and wisdom than the world e'er knew,
    Are darken'd with a film of stony hue.

There is no end to all my vain regret ;
    Even as the hopes were vast that in me grew,
So above all the hope of hope is set
A great despair that clings where life is lingering yet.

    I thought that this my well-belovèd son,
        My own sweet son, awful and beautiful,
Should be indeed the long-expected One,
        The true Messiah ; for the years were full,
        And though we trespass'd, God was pitiful ;
The land was weary of long widowhood,
        No error could God's promises annul,
And as I by my baby's cradle stood,
I sobb'd for very bliss, and prais'd the Lord of Good.

    Then, after, when He walk'd the grey hill-side,
        The olives seemed to glisten with bright life ;
Sweet music wander'd o'er the valley wide ;
        The birds were emulous in tuneful strife ;
        All earth and air with ecstasy were rife ;
The stars of evening glow'd with treble splendour,
        And crown'd those locks, where never came the
            knife,

With a pale glory, as they praise would render,
In their own silent way, to Israel's great Defender.

And God spoke to Him in mysterious ways,
    And taught Him in the wilderness strange lore ;
Yet was He full of sweet and humble grace,
    And duly all the homely duties bore ;
    But well I knew, the solemn smile He wore
Told of great thoughts we could not understand ;
    That other, nobler missions were in store
For such a heart as his, than with quick hand
To serve our daily wants, and ready waiting stand.

So when the call came, others ask'd and wonder'd ;
    But I remember'd what the angel said,
And how, when in my ears that message thunder'd,
    Desire and pride had cheer'd my heart, afraid ;
    So He went forth, and now is lying dead !
Dead with the hopes my faint heart deeply cherish'd ;
    How can I bear to dream that that dear head
Has bowed to Death, and all my faith e'er nourish'd
Of loyal, wise, and fair, with his pure breath has
      perish'd ?

How shall I spend the few, the sombre years

    That still must waste their tardy hours away ?

His memory shall in my embalming tears

    Find such a tomb as cannot know decay.

    The sharp distress of this eventful day

Shall linger on my old and weary heart,

    Till, all its pain by time worn dim and grey,

The older hopes shall once again find part

In all my thought and prayer, and never thence depart.

*   As she slowly moves away, the* ANGELS *resume :—*

CH. Surely these human wailings must arise

Into God's hearing like sweet symphonies ;

Not prayer itself can have more precious smell

Than frankincense of love made audible ;

But all their sorrow is confus'd and wild,

Like sobbings of a half-awakened child,

Who finds itself in silence of the night

Lorn of its mother, and despairs of light.

    SER. Thou wond'rest that they have so soon for-

        gotten

The living faith once in their hearts begotten ?

CH. Is it not strange?   Could *we* forget to bless
The gracious God in any wretchedness?
If His good pleasure for a while should doom
Our beauty to a dark and earthy tomb,
Would not what consciousness our brains still kept
Be praising still the love that never slept?
Can these have been with Jesus, and yet dream
That the cold earth contains Him?

SER.   Yea! I deem
The film of their mortality still covers ·
The glory from them where the new life hovers!
Were we as they are, clouds of doubt would hide
From us the light where now our souls abide.

CH. That can I feel,—for though my finer brain
Can reach a height their weakness may not gain,
Yet I myself am still too blind to see
What end to all this wonder there will be.
When, in the world's first morning, there was
    light,
And all the lucid air was calm and bright,
When Eden woke on Adam's opening eyes,

And God smil'd on his perfect Paradise,
E'en then the grating whine from Satan's lips
Clouded that beauty with a dun eclipse;
Elate with conquest, then he spread his sway
Over the earth, and man was forc'd obey;
For roses, thistles flourish'd; the pure sea
Grew salt and bitter with the poisonous tree
That bloom'd in Wormwood valley; Lust and Hate
Sprang up like weeds, and Love, disconsolate,
Flew on fair wings to heaven.   But all this pain
We knew would end in some benignant reign,
Where God's own loveliness should chase away
All spectral shadows from the clouded day.
This soul whose tomb we guard is surely He,
Whose coming caused the men of God to see,
From earliest ages through the night forlorn,
Sweet glimpses of the golden hope of morn.
But tell me, Seraph, wherefore has He died,
And how has our arch-foe been mortified,
Since He is dead who was both God and man?

SER.   The mysteries of time I dare not scan.
Yet this I know, the cunning fiend shall ache,

And for short triumph vaster anguish take,
From this brief life in death ; and Christ shall reign,
And in great glory rule the world again.
No more, in darkness and in vain despair,
Poor mortals shall from birth to death repair,
But, crown'd with laurels of redemption, they
From earth to heaven shall make a singing way.
For Christ, a man, where all men fail'd before,
Has learn'd the fulness of God's sacred lore,
And, in His dying, sinless, without stain,
Has made man spotless in God's sight again.
This miracle of grace shall be the praise
Of saints and angels through the endless days :
Even our holy wisdom cannot gauge
The worth of lowly man's vast heritage.
This glory, too, was won at no less price
Than Christ's humanity in sacrifice !
Behold a wonder ! can the King of kings,
Who breath'd the life into all moving things,
Succumb to death ?   Ah yes ! He bleeds, He dies !
But hear his whisper through those agonies,—
The echoes on from star to star are hurl'd,—
" I GIVE MY LIFE A RANSOM FOR THE WORLD ! "

But more than my poor tongue could e'er have spoken
You will have learn'd when this day's dawn has broken
And hush! e'en now far up in heaven I hear
The voice as of a rushing charioteer,
Who, through the empyrean in swift flight,
Heralds the coming of the Lord of Light!
This is the hour for which the expectant world
Through suffering ages, with long pinions furl'd
Over her gather'd limbs, with downcast eyes,
Has long'd for in her deepest agonies.
Now from this tomb where we have watch'd so long,
The Saviour rises with triumphant song,
And leaves behind him, in defeat and chains,
Sin and her doleful family of Pains,
For hark!   .   .   .   .

Far up in heaven the ARCHANGEL *proclaims silence.*

Blow ye the message on from star to star,
        Ye trumpet-winds afar!
Ye angels! from the crimson of whose wings
        Gold fire eternal springs,
Come from all corners of the dædal earth,
Come with a morning-singing, and make fair

The pinion-ploughèd air !
Ye prophets! still half-anguish'd with the birth
Of those great pæans of Jehovah's war
    Whose notes still echoing are,
Come with your sackcloth chang'd for robes of glory,
    And bow your grave locks hoary !
Ye saints and patient martyrs ' come ye all,
Come with sweet singing to our festival,
For Christ, who late hath in the cold earth lain,
    In triumph comes again !

*While the air rings with " Christ is risen," the two watchers rise
and meet the descending choir. As they hover in mid-air, their
song is heard above the harp-music.*

CHORUS.

    The morning light
    Has chas'd the night,
And the baleful shades of the dark take flight ;
    Our enamour'd eyes
    Have watch'd the rise
Of the Orb whose splendour fills the skies :
    We saw Him climb
    From the night of time
And truth burst forth in a golden prime.

This is the morn

When joy is born

To a sad world weary and faint and lorn ;

The bitter reign

Of hatred and pain

Is past, and Love is enthron'd again !

The frozen springs

Of all holy things

Are thaw'd with the warmth that the new light brings.

ANTI-CHORUS.

Ye isles of the West !

For ever caress'd

By the lulling swell of the Ocean's breast,

Your white-hair'd waves

And shadowy caves

Shall resound with the voice of a Truth that braves

The failing scorn

Of a priesthood born

In the lap of a worship old and worn.

The light that lies

Conceal'd from our eyes

In the depths of eternal destinies,
>> With wings unfurl'd
>> Shall sweep through the world
Till the powers of the dark to oblivion are hurl'd.
>> Ah! Lord Most High!
>> Let the years rush by,
Till the ultimate fulness of victory!

K

SONGS
AND SONNETS.

SONGS.

———•———

A LAMENT.

Sweet eyes, weep ye not for me,
Dim not lustre, which to see,
Now as in the days of old,
Days of love, sweet days of gold,
All revives of ancient rest
In this poor abandon'd breast.

Yet those lights of blue, oh! shroud
With each snowy veinèd cloud!
Drop adown thy golden hair;
Hide thy blushes, pure and fair;

Hold in nested peace that heart
Undisturbèd by my smart.

Worth hath long since fled from me,
Peace and joy and liberty ;
Self-contempt, whene'er I rise,
Lifting heavenward painèd eyes,
Bows me down, my brief glance turning,
Blind and sear'd with tears all burning.

Weep not, sigh not :—all is fled !
Love's full heart lies frozen dead ,
Shame with bitter lash aye scourges
All my mind's deep sea to surges,
O'er whose strife, with dead hopes strew'd,
Grim and battling vultures brood.

Memory only, 'mong the dead,
Open-eyed doth ceaseless tread
On the scattered bones that last,
White as moonlight, in the Past,
Answering all my backward gazing
By some pale ghost sadly raising.

Look up brightly ! there shall come
In the end some resting home,
Where in sleep unknown, unknowing,
Though the storms cease not their blowing,
'Mid Life's solemn sea, unhearing
I shall lie, and no thing fearing.

SONG FOR CORNELIA OVER MARCELLO.[1]

Hush! the sad sound of your weeping
Will awake my child from sleeping!
 Pluck me no more roses,
On the white brow lay a lily ;—
Which is flesh and which is flower?
 For both are chilly.
Leave me here alone an hour,
That I may deck my dear child's corse with posies.

Yet leave me not, for thoughts affright me!
Have you no other torch to light me,
 But this of funeral flaring?
Be silent! for we sleep together.

[1] In " Vittoria Corombona."

He is sleeping, I am dead;
My hair is white with wintry weather
  And frosty death, but his bright head
Its life of curls is wearing!

Forgive me, friends! my old brain wanders,
And mine is not the life Death squanders,—
  My boy is dead before me;
Yet leave me face to face with Death,
  For I must whisper in his ear
Some last maternal secrets, that I fear
  May perish with my faltering breath:
And when I lie on my last bed,
I fain would see my dear boy's head
  Smile and bend o'er me!

THE PARTING.

WE met within her silent home,
   With drooping gaze and inward sighing,
Dismay'd to find the moment come
   Which chang'd to weight our light replying,

While Poesy and Music mask'd
   With smiles the value of each minute,
To play us false our souls we task'd,
   And caroll'd light as spring-stirr'd linnet

False flew the notes across my ear,
   As strains unheeded o'er the ocean;
The troubled sea of mind saw near
   Naught but the spirit's wild emotion

And hymns of high heroic deed
　　Made reverent by some olden singer,
And Hope's bright sketch of glory's meed
　　Met no response to make them linger,

More eloquent as moments flew,
　　Within her passion-charmèd hearing,
And heavy on my lips then grew
　　The tales that once were all-endearing.

When all was o'er, and dumb we stood,
　　My soul went forth to hers unweeting,
At once immersèd in a flood
　　Of new-born love with one heart beating.

Ah! still methinks I see her stand,
　　Her love-fed soul her eyes o'erflowing,—
Still feel her cold and trembling hand,
　　That faintly press'd one all too glowing!

And did she feel? and did she love?
　　Ah, Heart, how vain thy doubting seemeth!
For all that night my soul did move
　　In starlit ways where Love's light gleameth.

Warm was my heart, my step elate,
    Although my walk was dark and lonely,—
On either fate, O Love, thou'lt wait,
    Though she and I be far friends only!

CAVALIER SONG.

MAIDEN, deign to wait and smile
On my suppliant lute awhile !
Surely when thy fragrant breath,
   Flying from its rosy gates,
Has such music in 't that Death,
   About to slay thy lover, waits,
And, overcome by strange surprise,
Seeks that music in thine eyes,—
Surely then my tender song
Can do your ling'ring ears no wrong !

Maiden, stay ! the hours flit by ;
At last a day will come to die ;

All men at last must let their hair
　With rosemary and yew be twin'd;
However brave they be and fair,
　Short time for pleasure they can find,
Oh! let them then at once be wise,
And fan the love-light in their eyes,
Before they lie in their cold home,
For there's no kissing in the tomb!

A FAIRY SONG.

ABOVE, above
In a light of love,
With white wings I move o'er the piny grove,
Uplit by the glory
Of Oberon's story,
Whose life like a beacon 's for ever before me ,
Whilst the purple-tipp'd mountain
Is solemn and still,
And the laurel-crown'd fountain
Sounds low from the hill.

For a summons from far
To these tree-tops hath come,
Like a voice from a star,
To my forest-roof 'd home,
As the faint day is falling
Into the green sea,

And Queen Mab is calling
     Her subjects to flee
All scenes sweet of slumber,
     By starlight to revel,
And come without number
     To trip on the level.

     As I fly, as I fly,
     I hear the faint sigh,
     With which mortal lover
     His passion doth cover ;
     As alone, as alone,
     With a tremulous groan,
In the depths of the forest, with a heart of the sore
     He maketh his moan.
     Then I let from my wing
     A drop of pure dew,
     With the balm of all Spring
     To fall on him true ;
     And lo! a faint motion
     The brambles among
     He hears with emotion ;—
     And she whom he sung

As the light of his eyes,
   The love of his heart,
To his bosom now flies,
   No more to depart.

And down the dark dell
   I skim to the cove,
And throw down a spell
   Of sleep on the dove;
And o'er the wide sea,
   So moonlit and still,
To Mab's islet I flee;—
   For such is her will.

O'er the sea, dimly lit
   By the round rising moon,
White wings I see flit,
   And shall be with them soon;
E'en now, like a star,
   Flashing o'er the white brine,
Is the faery-car
   Approaching the shrine!

L

Now the pearly sand
   Of the islet I view,
And the forest inland,
   And the lake so blue,
The cloud-crested mountains,
   The cedar-clad pass,
And the lawns and the fountains,
   Where grows the ring'd grass.

Now, mortals, farewell!
   No more may ye follow:
For each cavern and dell,
   Each hill-top and hollow,
Each high-spreading lawn,
   Each well and each river,
That that dim land adorn,
   Are sacred for ever!

A SONG OF THE NIGHT.

Good night! the silver veil of sleep
　　Will fall across our closèd eyes,
And our unconscious brains will keep
　　No careful memories.

If now the slumbrous soul forgets
　　The deepest passions it has felt,—
How, when the sun for ever sets,
　　Will earthly visions melt!

Good night! the crimson glow of morn
　　Will brighten o'er your waking face,
And I shall wake, alas! forlorn,
　　And run a shorter race.

Darker my dawning sure will be !
  The night of doubt is closing round :
The dim waves of Eternity
    Wash with a doleful sound !

Down the slope with flowers besprent
At noontide yesterday I went,
And some few precious hours I spent
    Beside the sounding sea;
The light-green wavelets at my feet
Upon the snow-white pebbles beat,
In oft-recurring music, sweet
    As moonlight melody;
The clouds were crimson-barr'd and gold,
Behind their crags I saw the old
Primeval blue its breadth unfold,—
    I saw it and was glad:
For no low-chanted lulling psalm,
No holy waft of Gilead balm,
Can bring my soul such stedfast calm,
    'Twould soothe a brain grown mad!

THE wild sobbing wind, and pale dying leaves,
    And cold damp mists, went flying
Around the old house, and under the eaves—
    And my Love, she lay dying!

A cold grey morning, and storm hush'd and still,
    Stars fading faint overhead;
A sigh, breathing love no sickness could kill,—
    And my sweet Love was dead!

SONNETS.

As when at sea, in storms and darkness drear,
    And distant far from sight of land or sky,
    We, overwhelm'd with weariness and fear,
    Feel dark despair on every heart doth lie;
When, 'midst the hollow booming of our gun,
    A light we see gleam in the murky air,
    And hail it as we would God's blessed sun,
    For help in our distress appeareth there;
So, when desponding thought doth me oppress.
    And painful doubt casts over me its chill,
    Thy spoken name, or sight of golden tress,
Or one dear scene anear a ruin'd mill,
    Doth cause the blinding tears of love to start,
    And faith in thine own truth to fill my heart.

II.

FROM CORNWALL.

Rarely, O Friend, in these "degenerate days,"
    Can we discover any hamlet rude,
    Where still the hush of pastoral solitude
    Is undisturb'd in seldom-trodden ways.
How sweet, then, while the winter wind delays
    To strip the beeches' solemn sisterhood,
    In some sweet western valley, where intrude
    No troubling sounds, and where no vulgar gaze
Can penetrate, to spend delicious hours
    Beside the ferny becks and torrent-streams,
    While fancy scales the cloud-embattled towers
Of Milton's empyrean, or sails wide
    Through Spenser's faery sea, or in the bowers
    Of Shakspeare's sonnets amorously doth hide !

III.

A JOY there is that yields me more delight,
 Hath o'er my soul a far intenser power,
 Than when, in ivy-crown'd and mossy bower,
 With roses wild and honeysuckle dight,
The rolling sea below, above the light
 Streaming full red through cloudy dome and
  tower,
 We claspèd hands in the sweet twilight hour,
 And pleading passion glowed with burning
  might !
Calm Joy ! thou bring'st a recollection dear,
 A sweeter, later day than that of Love,
 (Though words then spoken must for ever live),
When sneers and coldness lost their power to
  sear,
 When by sad Nature lifted far above,
 I knew the peace which she alone can give.

IV.

MEMORIES.

THE happy dwellers in green spring-tide valleys,
 The wanderers over moor and heath and down,
 Ladies of hill-tops far from any town,
 Where the fresh north wind o'er the grey wold
  sallies,
With antique garb, and old Greek songs out-
  singing,
 They come to bless me, shadows of the South,
 Sweet lily limbs, and dewy rose for mouth,
 And violet eyes from depths of soul upspringing ;
And some come crown'd with hyacinth and moly,
 A sad wan smile faint flickering on their lips,—
 Slowly they draw a veil of dim eclipse
Over their eyes so sweetly melancholy ;
 And some bring garlands dipp'd in mandragore,
 By moonlight pluck'd on some Circæan shore.

V.

WHAT man is there loves not the moon's white shell,
  Carv'd out upon the purple sky aright,
  When stars are waking in the early night,
  And flowers are closing up each tender bell
For dewy sleep? Ah! dear friend, loved so well!
  Thou, like the moon, didst borrow all thy light
  From the sweet source of glory and delight,
  The sun, my deity, my oracle!
Now for thy own sake art thou dear to me,
  For I have learn'd to find in all thy ways
  Peculiar beauty, where at first I saw
Only the lovely and reflected grace
  Of that pure soul who all through life must be
  My crown of comfort, my desire, and law.

VI.

A DAY IN THE INDIAN SUMMER.

Now Summer sweet, in beauteous form return'd,
  As loath to leave the scene of her delight,
  With saddest smile doth check the chilly night,
  From coldly stepping where her cheek had burn'd,
When as Apollo for her favour yearn'd ;
  He now at her doth gaze with failing might,
  Who, where the earth with yellow leaves is dight,
  Trembles to lose the knowledge she hath learn'd :
How sadly, with the shade of fleeting treasure,
  Across the solemn woods her spirit plays,
  Ling'ring o'er bowers, the olden haunts of pleasure,
That slowly fading die within the haze,
  The while they hear her dirge of soothing measure
  In one sweet dream forgetting buried days !

VII.

ON DUPONT'S "CHANSON HONGROISE."

WHAT southern scenes doth this sweet music waken,
    Such as rare Poussin most immortal made!
    —A full enjoyment 'neath the elm-tree shade;
    While from the luxury the hills have taken
A dreamy blue, as if on them were shaken
    A mantle dim, lest all green things should fade
    Beneath so fierce a sun!—Now youth and maid
    Have joyfully the sunny vines forsaken,
To meet, where, lo! under the spreading trees
    A shepherd piping sits beside a river;
    And then succeed the laugh, and dance, and song,
With such a whirl that all their spirits quiver!—
    Oh! nowhere couldst thou find, those hearts among,
    One whose young blood a chilling fear did freeze!

VIII.

As if two, wandering through a garden fair,
   In whose green heart a high-wall'd palace lay,
   Should try this door and that to find a way,
   And, finding none, should walk contented there,
Until one turn'd aside to pluck a rare
   High-twining rose, and, coming back to say
   How sweet the alley blossom'd where it lay,
   Should find her sister vanish'd unaware ;
Yet, by a murmur of doors shut within,
   Should know that to the palace she was led,
   And yet should wail for sorrow, and begin
To weep in passion for her unseen friend,—
   Such is their woe who mourn the happy dead,
   And will not wait in patience for the end.

IX.

TO PERCY BYSSHE SHELLEY,

WHOSE SPIRIT HAUNTS ALL PINE-WOODS AND SEA-SOLITUDES
IN ENGLAND AND ITALY.

AMID these pines, in which, though bright the sky,
 A solemn stillness creeps as in the tomb,
 A blissful calm, a soul-subduing gloom,
 Save that the light, when ocean breezes sigh
Through parted boughs, gleams golden from on high,—
 Amid these ruin'd walls and beauties wild
 Of ivy dark in ferny dells beguil'd,
 O lost and gentle one, I feel thee nigh !
Thy song intense with thrilling music's chaunted
 Adown the shore and on the pine-clad hill,
 From all cool nooks by lightsome spirit haunted ;
And peaceful thoughts, though sad, my breast do fill,
 When as beyond these boughs I view our sea,
 Pine-crown'd and blue as thine in Italy !

X.

WITH A BIRTHDAY GIFT OF WEBSTER'S PLAYS.

Poet and Friend! Pause while the bells of Time
   Ring out this great division of your days,
   And let the cadence of these sombre lays
   Be the grave echo of their silver chime ,
And as you slowly up to glory climb,
   Nigh fainting in the lower thorny ways,
   Take solace from th' eternal wreath of bays
   That crowns at last this weary brow sublime ;
His was a soul whose calm intensity
   Glared, shadeless, at the passion-sun that blinds,
   Unblinded, till the storm of song arose ;—
Even as the patient and Promethean sea
   Tosses in sleep, until the vulture winds
   Swoop down and tear the breast of its repose.

XI.

A PICTURE.

SHE tapp'd her scarlet slipper listlessly
   Against the hollow rushes on the floor,
   And twined a rose, deep crimson to the core,
   Among the golden waving luxury
Of her loose hair; an orange-girdled bee
   Raised with his boisterous song of honey-lore
   'Her languid eyes, that idly watch'd before
   The sunlight creeping upward to her knee :
A step came suddenly upon the stair,
   A firm foot from the silence climbing higher :—
   The sound woke all her wan face to a flush ;
Down slipp'd the rose-bud from her floating hair :—
   A pause while every feature flash'd with fire :
   Then love met love in one entrancing rush !

XII.

ENGLAND IN ITALY.

1.

"How oft of late my fever'd gaze I've lifted
  Morn after morn o'er olives, dusky green,
  Up this intensity of blue to glean
One homeless cloud that may have slowly drifted
From lands rain-mantled and with verdure gifted!"
  —Thus did I moan; and that same eve was seen
  A dark and purple cloud float o'er the screen
Of rosy mist that wrapp'd the mountains rifted:
What strength doth lie in quietude, what might
  Rests peacefully beneath the raving thunder!
  Next morn pale clouds, in wild and weird affright,
Fled fast in ghastly guise the wan moon under,
  Yet view'd I, 'neath the glare of flashing light,
  Snowfields a-sleeping in that scene of wonder.

XIII.

ENGLAND IN ITALY.

2.

So, in the deep enjoying of thy heart,
　Thy heart of passion-warmth, O Italy !
　Thy grand possession of the soul of Art,
　Thy mountains echoing Shelley's minstrelsy,
'Midst all the bliss and glow and inspiration,
　The eternal spring, the radiancy of health,
　That stirred me with a fierce intoxication,
　Escaping from my lips as if by stealth,
One faint low sigh arose from off the altar
　Of my pure worship, e'en while at thy lips
　Thy plenitude I drew in, kiss by kiss ;
O faithful Heart ! sweet darkener of my bliss !
　Thy one poor sigh made dear the chill eclipse
　That bared the past and made my passion falter.

XIV.

ENGLAND IN ITALY.

3.

I stood in Pisa, in that Holy Field,
   On whose rough walls Orcagna drew strange things,
   Picturing Dante's weird imaginings,
   Of all that Heaven and Hell were forced to yield
To his all-conquering soul, whose prelude flew,
   Like some large night-bird of unhealth and woe,
   Across the drear morass of Time's dull flow,
   And bloom'd, ere death thrice bless'd with vision true,
A song of Paradise full glorified !—
   Ah ! ghastly showed the sculptures, ghastly pale,
   Beneath the moon, the paved way long and lone ;
And wearily my yearning utterance died.
   Oh ! sweet then, Love, thy violets English blown,
   New gather'd in a pleasant western vale !

XV.

LADIES' TRESSES.

INSCRIBED TO M. C. AND J.

THE dear one we both love so well, and I,
  Climb'd yesterday along the red hill-side,
  Over the flat green tufts of moor-grass, dried
  With the fierce sunlight of an August sky,
Until we gained the ledges grey that lie
  Round the sheer summit; as my eye glanc'd wide
  O'er the tumultuous slope of grass, I spied
  A little spiral whiteness, not more high
Than a mole's shoulder. 'Twas sweet ladies' tresses;
  Soon in her hand the gather'd flow'ret lay,
  And in the dreamy autumn light that blesses
The distant woods with shades of grey and blue,
  We spoke of one who was so far away,
  And wished our flow'ret had been pluck'd by you.

XVI.

THE RIVER PENPONT.

I SIT so still upon the river-brink ;
   The trout float underneath me leisurely ;
   The great green dragon-flies swoop down to drink,
   And plume their gauze wings on the ferns hard by ;
Weird shadowy beeches towards each other bend
   Across the bosom of the twinkling stream,
   Whence honeysuckle-garlands faintly send
   Rich perfume felt like music in a dream ;
The sunlight through the canopy of leaves
   In starry fretwork gilds the watery floor :
   In all this summer weather nothing grieves,
Except the stream that murmurs to the moor,—
   Except the stream and I, who cannot borrow,
   Light from my sweet Love's eyes to banish sorrow.

XVII.

"FROM DEATH UNTO LIFE."

1.

AMID this night of woe I heard a voice,
  Far, far beyond the sea of pleasure sweet,
  Whose kindling waves my lips did hotly meet,
  That sounded in my ears, " Rejoice! rejoice!"
Within the young spring-time ; and all the joys
  That I had vowed to shun, and Passion's heat
  Rising and surging with tumultuous beat,
  Fled far away mix'd with the world's rude noise ;
And I arose a man, sin-bound though strong,
  Thinking God's messenger had come reproving,
  When lo ! abash'd, I viewed a form among
The lilied fields in radiant glory moving,
  Who cried "The Spring hath dawn'd ! —prepare
      thy song,
  For I thy Light am here, unlov'd though loving."

XVIII.

"FROM DEATH UNTO LIFE."

2.

HE walk'd by running waters, and the light,
From snowy lilies in that narrow way,
Upon his wounded feet did softly play,
Trembling beneath his ever-drooping sight:
Oh! how his lowliness did put to flight
My lofty thoughts in realms where proud souls
stray,
The while his voice upon my spirit lay
Unresting in an all o'er-coming might!
I went into the primrose fields and wept;
I could but weep to think of his dear love;
And soon a wond'rous lightness o'er me crept,
A peace not quiet all, but that did move
My clay-cold heart that erst in gloom had slept,
To hymn my wingèd soul to fields above.

XIX.

"FROM DEATH UNTO LIFE."

3.

THOUGH now to me the fleeting days are stored
  With thoughts of highest bliss most pure and
      true,
  That Faith the frail from Hope's fair painting drew,
  Dismay and Doubt have oft upon me pour'd
Their power and spell with bitter dart and sword,
  Like that dread storm which o'er the waters blue
  Of Galilee's fair lake in horror grew,
  And made faint souls in fear to awake their Lord ;
But He, whom His humanity so press'd
  That then as man He slept, sleeps now no more,
  And with this faith gives us a present rest.
Though other tempests hurl their sullen roar,
  They sully not the peaceful haven blest
  He gain'd for us with so much anguish sore.

XX.

A MADONNA IN THE ANTWERP MUSEUM.

INSCRIBED TO J. F. B

THROUGH the long centuries comes faint and dim
   The blast of trumpets and the brazen clang
   That from the seventh Charles's bastions rang,
   When France went out, armed or in merry trim ;
And we forget the feats of state and war
   That thrill'd the heroes of the elder age,
   Taking their conquests for our heritage,
   Nor grateful to the men that fought afar ;
And yet our hearts are open'd when we see
   (All thanks to Jehan Foucquet) through the years
   Sweet Agnes Sorel of the noble heart
And the wise face, and hear all suddenly
   Down the world's silence the slow-falling tears
   On the grey tomb where a king mourns apart !

XXI.

ANSTEY'S COVE.

INSCRIBED TO W. A. P.

WALTER, when through the thirsty streets and squares
    Of London, in the burning sun of June,
    We wander, and the too-melodious tune
    Of barrel-organs chafes us unawares,
What would we give to rise on sudden wings,
    And fly where southward lay our mutual home,
    Where in the rock-pools boils the smitten foam,
    Or where from corn-fields soars the lark and sings !
One day shall be to us for ever dear,
    When on the quarried margin of the shore
    We sat with the sea-music in our ear,
Until the solitude our spirits bore
    Into sweet depths of thought, where grief and fear
    Sank, and were drown'd in love to rise no more !

XXII.

TO DEVON.

1.

GREAT Guardian of the dim unfathom'd West!
  O Thou whose vast and rugged heart is set
  'Mid storm-swept moorlands where thou dost beget
  The battling hail and whirlwind!　In thy quest,
Borne on the lone upheavings of thy breast,
  A cloud I've wander'd where the clouds are met
  Close-clasping peaks fantastic in the fret
  Of rain-drift breaking o'er each granite crest!
Strength hath, O Spirit! in thy heart his home,
  Rough and ungarnish'd; yet in what sweet guise
  Thou dost the springtime bless! from out the dome
Of what blue depths dost thou with tender eyes
  O'erlook new flower-births, and, where zephyrs roam,
  Make dark moors lovely under summer skies!

XXIII.

TO DEVON.

2.

As some proud mistress whose unweeting scorn
  Disdains the heart that sigheth in her thrall,
  And thinks of him, if so she think at all,
  As thronèd queen might think of beggar born ;
Yet he, the while in secrecy and pain,
  By reason of the intensity of love,
  Will never from his mind her thought remove,
  And, past all rescue, holds his soul in chain;
So, though, dear land, alas ! we parted are
  By many leagues of meadow, vale, and hill,
  And thou art all regardless of my care,
Yet thoughts of thee do my sad bosom fill,
  And in my dreams I tread thy solemn shores,
  Thy blissful shadowy woods, and purple moors.

XXIV.

INSCRIBED TO I. L. T. B.

S<small>AD</small> and alone and weary, nigh despairing,
   I sat in the old church above the sea,
   And heard the organ sound a peal of glee,
   Like some great solemn " bird of God" declaring
Peace and good-will to all who, meek robes wearing,
   Hail'd the bright dawning advent ; but for me
   There was no comfort till that minstrelsy
   Had faded, and the silent air was bearing
One sweet clear voice, that said, " Unto Me come,
   Ye heavy-laden ! unto Me, and I
   Will bear your burden !"   Then my terror ceased,
And, gazing out, I saw, across the foam,
   God's symbol smite along the wintry east,
   Pale gold between the waters and the sky.

DEVONIANA.

HOLNE CHACE.

How strange it is to pace some olden haunt,
Unvisited since childhood's blithe desire
Led the same feet through half-familiar paths
To the lov'd spot for frolic or for rest,—
How strange to find in each grotesque detail
Of twisted trunk, or mossy boulder-stone,
A form laid up in corners of the brain,
And often ponder'd over ! strange to feel
The early buoyancy of restless mirth
No longer forcing the o'er-venturous steps
To clamber vainly down the perilous gorge
In search of ferns and flowerets !   Then the morn,
Glittering and cold, seem'd most delightful time
For these swift visits ; now the quiet eve,

And noiseless ending of the afternoon,
Please most the calm and meditative mind.
Hence with full heart, in this wild bower, arch'd o'er
With twining ivy and the traveller's joy,
I sit this summer evening and review
The short May-day of passion and of thought
Men call my life, and ponder on the ways
Of God, who leads us by an inner voice
Oracular, through ways we dream'd not of,
And new-creates ambition in our souls,
And gives us power to fashion, or makes known
Our weakness to us ;—lessons manifold
That pierce our hearts like lightning, and appear
To outward show in laughter or in tears.

O solemn ceaseless river, that dost flow
In darkness through the valley at my feet !
Judge me not arrogant if now at last,
After so many days, I seek again
To mingle my faint song of love and praise
With all the pastoral tribute of long years !
How, since the earliest dawn of life and warmth
In the young earth primæval, hast thou heard

Praises from all thy banks !   Around thy source
Grey-headed hills bow down in mute amaze,
Reverent and hush'd, while here the obsequious woods
Bend o'er thy current, and the fragrant stars
Of blackthorn and of may fall noiselessly
Into thy breast as incense from the Spring.
Surely thou hast a spirit of keen life,
Whose amorous sway binds all the winds and flowers,
And brooding birds, and all things blithe and young,
Into a rapt fraternity of praise !
Alas ! that human eyes should be so dull !
I only cannot see what every bird,
The very flowers, are glorified in seeing ;—
I cannot hear when in melodious choir
The hymn of Nature rises ;—all I feel
Is that the dew seems fresher by thy banks,
And that the music of thy twinkling stream
Makes my heart bound more gladly !

Yet perchance
It is my deeper love for thee that frames
These dreams of general worship ; thou hast been
My sponsor into song, for thou didst take

My rhyming vows upon thee, when as yet
The faltering tongue lack'd skill to round a verse;
And, O majestic stream! didst teach me lore,
Whether of music, or of hue or form,
Such as no other teacher could have taught.

Hence, with a reverent heart and full of thanks
To Him who dower'd my childhood with such wealth
Of pure delights and natural influence,
I come to listen once again, O Dart!
To thy great voice beneath me in the glen;
And through my brain comes rushing with new awe
The tragic story of thy fierce revenge,
That chill'd my blood in earlier, younger years.
Cruel thou wert, O river! but not for that
Can I revoke my love ; rather condemn
The heedlessness of those unhappy ones!
Short is the tale, but sad !—It was the spring,
When the bright heats of April had made warm
The heap'd-up snow around thy chilly springs,
Which melting in the sunshine, suddenly,
Along the streamlet-bed and through the glens,
The floods came fiercely dashing to the sea.

Two brothers, one a dweller in these vales,
The other late return'd from weary years
Under a tropic sun, had met at last,
With such a calm delight as grown men feel,
In the south city of the gleaming masts.
Now back again the elder brother brought
Another son home to the gray old dame
That spun and waited in her cottage home
(To wait, alas! till Heaven should give her peace);
They, weary with the endless burning moor,
Were resting on that meadow at my feet.
There, while they loll'd upon the close warm grass,
Hard by the mossy pillars of the bridge,
Half-dozing in the lassitude of heat,
And dreaming of the flow of happy years
That were to be, and peace, and calm repose,
And hum of bees, and distant low of kine,
And caw of rooks in solemn quiet elms,
And sweet sedge-warblers singing of true love,—
All flowing round the dulcitude of love,—
Suddenly, with a sharp tumultuous roar,
A gurgling rushing noise of many streams
Came down the wild ravine; and round the glen,

Frothy and brown, like a gigantic wall,
The flood came right upon them.

                    This strange tale,
True in the pity of a hundred hearts,
Came to my boyish ears ere yet the sight
Of human suffering taught me human love,
And made the spell of thy wild loveliness
A passion to me ; beautiful thou wert,
And now I knew thee swift and strong to smite,
And weirdest admiration filled my heart.

And now adieu ! within the hateful whirl
Of city-strife, and when the weariness
Of a slow circular life shall pain me most,
Thy cool luxuriance, and the lapping sound
Of currents rushing through the mossy stones,
Shall oft sustain me !   O immortal stream !
Thy blessed memory helps me to sustain
A steady front to all the blows of Fate;
And now I leave thee, stronger for this hour
Of deep communion with the all-wise heart
Of Nature beating in this mossy valley.

A DAY-DREAM.

ADDRESSED TO M. H. C.

LAST night, methought, dear friend, when sudden
    paus'd
The night-wind's maddening race across the bay,
With rain and lightning pale, and wailings sad
About the shelter of new-budded trees,
Methought, amid a pause, a silence deep,
Sudden and strange, that that sweet time which we
Had promis'd to ourselves in fondest hope,
One mild May-morn, by parting clouded o'er,
Had sudden come in bright effulgence rare,
And lo ! we two had met to wander, glad,
Alone, and free, in deep Devonian lanes.

The few short months, with all their city-life,
Their time made torture, and their joys made sad,
By bitter recollection and the thought

That draws comparison, stood not within
The deepest subtle cell of memory ;
Blank was the time, and yet I knew 'twas gone,
E'en as I stood within those lanes with thee ;
For golden mists now hid and now reveal'd
The dim obscurity of moorland hills ;
And trees of old acquaintance, well-belov'd,
Whose very outline was a source of joy,
Showed alter'd hue of yellow, pale and wan,
Against the haze of warm September skies.

Yet must that time have been ; but mystery all,
Dark, drear, and unaccountable it seem'd ;
Vainly I strove, and evermore in vain,
To wring from out the past, which, like a den,
Distant and black and vast, o'er-lowering stood,
One faint remembrance, though of weary strife,
Of joy, aye-sought, unfound ;—but silence all
The dull immensity enwrapp'd and held.

How strange, and yet how sweet ! for who would have
The balm and magic of the Autumn calm,
All the infinitude of landscape quiet

In somnolence outstretch'd, disturb'd and vex'd,
Take hasty hues unfix'd, fickle and gay
As lightsome April laughing in the breeze?
Yet so Remembrance would have work'd among
These pleasures pure by hinting of the Past,
Ill-spent and lost and irrecoverable.

Again with thee! ah, whither shall we turn
Our willing steps?—to the lone sea, mist-hid
And mildly gentle to its lonelier shore,
Where echoes scarce are heard, so calm the waves,
And only heard because the calm on land
Is wrapp'd in silence deeper,—or shall we
In hill and dale a greater glory find?

Then did we wander forth, the ocean leaving,
A twinkling line, uncertain, wavering, far,
For I did name an orchard-nested spot,
The haunt of black-caps that awaken morn
With glorious depths of melody full-toned,
Like falling waters in a mellow song,
Not all unworthy sweetest Philomel,
Love-sick and pining in an Eastern grove.

Here, face to face with Quiet, soon we found
That we were also heart to heart with her.
It was a hollow dell by trees o'erhung,
With rich excess of fruit shot through the green,
Yellow and red and streak'd like summer morn.
Ere long we rose, oppress'd by all the weight
Of interlacing boughs and nestling leaves
Down-stooping towards long grass, the ceaseless hum
Of laden bees across the scented air,
And strip of blue minute above the trees :
So down a winding hill-side lane (a lane
With faint airs heavy and by heights enclosed)
We moved, until a sudden turn revealed
Unto our verdure-charmèd eyes a gleam,
Dazzling and white, of water stretching wide
Unto a shore beyond ; and here expanse
Gave plenty unto feasting Fancy's eye.
The shore, half cliff, and partly grassy bank,
Most pleasantly o'erlook'd the waters clear,
Oft-times so near the path, that swimming fish,
Catching reflection strange, with startling dart
Would sudden vanish into deep dark pools ;
And nigh unto the stream,— the cool Teign head,—

A group of damsels and of youths just fresh
From apple-harvest, in a meadow cool'd
By elms and river-breathings, sat in rings,
With song and dance and junkets—fittest food
For dainty pixies in a mossy cave!
O happy Pastoral! enjoyment rare!
And mirth and gladness, innocent yet high!
How was 't that here, in such a sunny spot,
'Mid such a glee and such a merry mood,
That first a shade, solemn and all too deep,
Crept o'er the lightness of my spirit glad?
I knew not then;—for still the autumn sun
Gleam'd bright and clear and high within the west;
Still gleam'd the waters, stricken by his ray,
And pleasurably twinkled; still bright clouds
Through veil-like shades adown the happy hills,
Sloping in quietude to quiet waves;
Yet all my inward soul, my spirit's life,
Which lives within the life, the life of all,
Threw out a fear at sight of young delight,
An apprehension wan that coloured all
Around me and above with sadden'd hue.
And onward down that quiet shore we went,

Mute and dismay'd, with eyes that search'd each hedge
For fern and flower, until a haze appear'd
That o'er the river mouth moved slow to sea,
A haze of smoke of town or fishing nook,—
And then in gazing at the whole extent
Of sunlit land that form'd the other shore,
Two villages, in shelt'ring hills held sweet,
Awaken'd by their names the sudden thought,
Which half-aloud I spake with bounding heart,
That *this is Keats's land !*—but when we came
Unto a little bay, a valley deep,
Wooded, and beauteous in a vista long
Of many shades and colours glorious,
Fill'd us with solemn silence ; and the sound
Of soft and silvery waters bubbling slow,
Coming beneath a bridge, one simple arch
That seem'd more moss than stone, there was no need
To name it,—*Archbrook !*   Hours we lingered there,
Till eve threw dusky shadows o'er our path,
Yet ne'er before was I so moved, so dumb
With feeling's large excess ;—the man, his life
Tumultuous in passion agoniz'd,
His strains matur'd in immaturity,

His swift short life, his strange and lonely death,
All came to me in portraiture so clear,
So vivid and entire, that anguish seiz'd
My soul, though dry my eyes, though full my heart,
And all my being seem'd to pass to his
Within the strength of sympathetic thought.
And all that sky,—its crimson western bars
Stretching athwart the horizon's green and gold,
Distinct and radiant above the hills,—
The dark blue east, cloudless and pure, and all
The depths of waters, river-banks, and sound
Of brooklet rushing, evermore are fix'd
Within my mind ;—that selfsame sky to be,
With all that wealth of hill and dale and stream,
A guide unfailing to the thought of Keats!

THE END.

Printed in the USA
CPSIA information can be obtained
at www.ICGtesting.com
LVHW011451070724
784843LV00013B/932